Kaleidoscope View
of a Mad Mad World

By

Martin Olson

as told to: Peter Mars

This book is a work of non-fiction. Names and places have been changed to protect the privacy of all individuals. The events and situations are true.

ISBN: 1-4107-7267-5 (e-book)
ISBN: 1-4107-7266-7 (Paperback)

Library of Congress Control Number: 2003095265

This book is printed on acid free paper.

Printed in the United States of America
Bloomington, IN

1stBooks – rev. 08/22/03

FOREWORD

I have taken the liberty of condensing a work of history that has been out of print for sixty years and is currently unavailable, yet one that deserves to be looked at carefully. The original researchers, Frederick L. Schuman and George D. Brodsky, in their book, *Design for Power*, found a unique comparison between the wars, which took place throughout the first half of the twentieth century, and the children's story of *Alice in Wonderland*. I was so impressed by this work that I felt it necessary to reconstruct it and to add to it the conflicts that have continued during the latter half of that period and into the new millennium.

My purpose in writing *Kaleidoscope* is to show that society never seems to change throughout all generations. As I looked back to *The History of the Rise and Fall of the Roman Empire* and continue forward to this day and age, I discover that, even with the remarkable advances that have transpired over the last century, we are no further ahead in our societal ways of solving problems or of handling situations than we were two-thousand years ago.

I have also included some personal observations and experiences from my work and travel throughout the world as a means to explain further the importance of knowing and understanding the events that have taken place and how those events have mysteriously reoccurred in one form or another over the years, proving that history does, in fact, repeat itself.

Martin Olson

INTRODUCTION

A kaleidoscope is a tubular optical instrument in which loose pieces of colored glass are enclosed at one end of the tube and are reflected in mirrors so as to display ever changing symmetrical patterns as the tube is rotated and the pieces shift within the enclosure.

That is also a just description of a mad, mad world that is, likewise, a maze of continually shifting patterns as evidenced by the ever-changing governments formed by the loose bits of society that control each country.

FROM THE AUTHOR...

I published a book in 2002 entitled *Iron Shoes* in association with Peter Mars. This non-fiction chronicle relates the personal journey I took in my work and the travels I made throughout the world. That work encompassed my occupation as a builder of shopping centers, and as a director of real estate and development for Sears Roebuck and Company's eastern territory as well as for the Hilton Hotel chain. It included working with Clark Clifford of Washington, DC and former US President Richard M. Nixon. It involved travels in various countries in Europe and Africa as I was employed by an operative of the Central Intelligence Agency, the United Nations, and finally as assistant to the chairman of a Swiss trust.

These became the roads of my life and all of them eventually took me into totally different directions, none of which were by my choice. I always looked ahead and never looked back. The roads just seemed to always be there for me even when obstructions confounded me or blocked my way. There were always detours that allowed me to continue onward.

It was important to me that I document, before I died, my journey with a special emphasis on the problems I encountered with Richard Nixon. I needed to impart my knowledge of what he did as a lawyer for Japan and as a Vice-president for the United States. This was my focus in writing *Iron Shoes*.

Recently, I was invited to the studios of Channel 9 in Augusta, Maine to be interviewed on a television program in which *Iron Shoes* became the central topic. In the course of my discussion with the host, Katy Perry, she asked me my thoughts on the current political situation concerning Iraq and North Korea. I replied that if the genie ever comes out of the bottle it will never be able to be put back in the bottle. Her question to me was, "Who is the genie?" That was not an easy question to answer because I wanted to find one word that would adequately suffice as a reply. That answer was not a "who" but "what." The genie is "hatred." It feeds the soul of many people globally and once it has taken hold, it cannot be erased for generations. Although the majority of religions in the world hold to the basic tenets of love, charity and kindness to others, many do not practice what they preach.

The proof of what I have discovered about this genie can be seen in a book I found recently when I was vacationing with my wife in Greenville, Maine. I happened to go to the Greenville Library where a book sale was in progress. There I found a book that was well over fifty years old entitled, "Design for Power – The Struggle for the World" by Frederick L. Schuman and George D. Brodsky. I purchased the book for fifty cents after reading a few chapters. The book amazingly detailed the major countries that had some part in World War I and World War II and how each of them became involved in these wars. I was familiar with much of this as I had exposed in *Iron Shoes* similar occurrences in which deals are made by governments and political games are a way of doing business. *Design for Power* gave added credibility to the fact that all governments and people basically operate the same way.

Because I have lived through many of the changes that have taken place during this period I am more than familiar with these events. And as I reflect back upon all that I have read about in history and have witnessed in my lifetime, I become more and more convinced that our world is truly a kaleidoscope that makes everything look well-balanced when one glances through the eyepiece but, when there is further investigation, it is shown to be a disturbing jumble of broken bits and shards, a mirror image of the corrupt governments that have existed for millennia.

"We may be pretty certain that persons whom all the world treats ill deserve the treatment they get. The world is a looking glass and gives back to every man the reflection of his own face. Frown at it, and it will in turn look sourly upon you; laugh at it and with it, and it is a jolly, kind companion; and so let all young persons take their choice." Thackery

TABLE OF CONTENTS

CHAPTER ONE – JAPAN

"There's glory for you!" "I don't know what you mean by 'glory,'" Alice said. Humpty Dumpty smiled contemptuously. "Of course you don't – till I tell you. I meant, 'there's a nice knock-down argument for you!'" "But 'glory' doesn't mean 'a nice knock-down argument,'" Alice objected. "When I use a word," Humpty Dumpty said in a rather scornful tone, "it means just what I choose it to mean – neither more nor less." "The question is," said Alice, "whether you can make words mean so many different things." "The question is," said Humpty Dumpty, "which is to be Master – that's all." [1]

* * * * *

I am at an age where I can recall, not only stories told to me, but first-hand knowledge about the time when Japan came forward from its status as a feudal kingdom of monks and armored knights to become a great nation of industrialists and bankers with great power in the western Pacific. For a country with no available natural resources, it progressed from a medieval empire with no desire to be corrupted by European or American ways of life, to a land in which its people were forced to accept Western means and inventions. From the time when Commodore Matthew Perry sailed into Tokyo Bay with letters and gifts, and instructions from Washington, DC, he put pressure on the Japanese people to sign a treaty with the United States allowing for the opening of Japanese ports to American merchants. Once this was established, other countries made equal demands upon these people.

Feuding clans in Japan, which had remained rivals for centuries, now had greater challenges. The unchanging stoic ways of the immoral Tokugawas was being threatened by the desires for advancement and development of new ideas by their opposing clans, the Satsumas and the Choshus. These latter two clans saw the wisdom in adopting Western ways and by exercising their power made great strides in their country by adopting many of the ideas of the newcomers. Following this path, Japan would not allow itself to succumb to their greatest enemy, China, who continually threatened Japan's shores. By allying itself with the Western world, it would keep China at bay as the Chinese did not want to face the wrath of the world's most powerful nation, even at that time. The Japanese furthered their standing as a state when they began to copy all of the electrical, electronic and mechanical devices that were manufactured in the United States and that gave America enormous wealth as a result of its creative acumen. Once Japan entered this new way of life, it began its journey to becoming a great power.

As in the *Alice in Wonderland* excerpt, Japan wanted now to be 'Master' of all. After trading with the United States and being supplied with the Western tools of war, Tokyo's governing body looked toward the mainland of Asia with a desire to conquer and own all the land it encompassed. Following the lead of the ancient Japanese warlords, Tokyo invaded Korea and eventually China. In less than a year both Korea and Manchuria were overrun. In order to maintain some semblance of peace, China made a deal with Japan. Japan demanded $150,000,000 and the ownership of Formosa, the

Pescadores Islands, and the Liaotung Peninsula, key to Manchuria. Because China was an important trading center to many of the Western powers, Russia, Germany and France intervened and forced Japan to give up the Liaotung Peninsula, thereby stopping Japan in its quest for expansion. Japan did not like being stepped on in this manner and determined to prepare itself to defy the Western powers if Japan was to tear apart and acquire a significant portion of a helpless China.

In the early part of the twentieth century, Japan had built up its military forces under Admiral Togo enough so that it went into battle at sea against Russia. Russia was no match for the new Japanese fleet as its squadrons were destroyed and Japan captured Port Arthur and re-acquired the Liaotung Peninsula. In a treaty signed at Portsmouth, New Hampshire, Japan was given the Russian railway along with mining rights in South Manchuria as well as the southern half of the Island of Sakhalin.

Japan was regaining its Master's status and entered into pacts with Paris and St. Petersburg opening the way for it to become a partner in the Triple Entente.

Several islands in the Pacific had been under German control for a number of years, having been bought from Spain. Japan, in its master plan, seized these territories for its own after communicating with Germany and demanding that Berlin withdraw its warships from the Far East. When Germany did not respond, Japan declared war and forced a German retreat.

Japan then took advantage of a revolution that was occurring in Russia by invading Siberia. Once again Tokyo was aggravating the Western powers causing friction with the United States. But Japan was on a mission to secure for itself additional land. It was already supreme in eastern Asia and nothing was going to stop its continuing conquests.

Japan had become the third greatest naval power behind Britain and the United States.

At the Paris Peace Conference and, later, at the Four Power Pacific Pact, which included Washington, London, Paris and Tokyo, a series of treaties were signed wherein each agreed to respect their rights in relation to their possessions and dominions in the Pacific region. They further agreed to consult with one another should any threat of aggression arise.

As Japan continued to build internally, and merchandising and money-making became a part of its goals, the American Great Depression interrupted financial stability for all who had maintained trade with the United States. This created insecurities in Japan and led, as elsewhere, to political fanaticism including a resurgence of militant imperialism. Bankers and businessmen had dominated a capitalism, which was already monopolistic rather than competitive. These men used their influence over the ruling politicians but they could not compete with the real rulers of the land, the professional specialists in violence.

For centuries in feudal Japan, the lords of the land who were called the Daimyo, and the Samurai who commanded their peasant troops, held the ultimate power. In the new Japan, all the power went to the army, which had retained its inspiration from the days of the Samurai but were now equipped with the modern machines of war. Unlike the wealthy aristocracy with their political connections, the army was comprised of the youth who had come from poor and humble origins. Most had a great devotion to the Emperor and to the polytheistic Shinto religion, and most had contempt for the businessmen, the bankers and the politicians.

These militaristic men felt that politicians did not use the correct methods for the establishment of peace. Armies and navies exist for war. Wars are fought to establish peace. Whoever opposes war is, therefore, the enemy of peace and a traitor to the Emperor. It became an accepted practice that any patriotic officer that might be confronted by disgrace was to commit *hara-kiri* to save face and the honor of his ancestors. Equally, should a patriotic officer see others disgracing his nation, they too should be put to death.

The new army, disgusted with the easy-going reasonableness of the existing politicos, were insulted by their lack of patriotism so they decided to act. Their plan was simple: they would murder all the ministers opposed to army rule, along with any officers they deemed to be uncooperative. In February of 1936, a number of regiments, including the Imperial Guard, began seizing public buildings in Tokyo. One by one, they put to death those they had determined to be enemies within the state.

As the time for renewal of the naval treaties arrived, Tokyo demanded naval parity with Britain and America. London and

Washington refused. Tokyo then declined to renew its position and withdrew its delegates from the conference. Immediately Japan made plans to build more warships. There was no doubt, although it was not known for sure, that Japan wanted a war. They chose China as their victim. It would easily be won as Japan believed that China could be subdued at little cost or risk. Their reasoning was that China was stirring with new life and a war for 'peace' would rally all Japan behind the warlords. The army's goal was to keep China divided and Japan united. China was vulnerable as it had internal strife created by the opposition of those of its people who followed Communism and those others who followed Christianity as embraced by their leader, General Chiang Kai-shek. The General was backed by China's bankers and had allied himself with the landlords and men of money. This added to the division within China as struggles ensued with the strife of classes among the General's followers. Open violence broke out and in order to keep control against the poorer masses, he made himself a tyrant.

A civil war started but was to last only long enough to weaken China even further. The strange end to the civil strife came about when the General and the leader of the Communists, Chou En-Lai, agreed that it was more important to have unity than vengeance.

In mid-August 1937 the invasion of China was launched. Thousands upon thousands of men, women and children were slaughtered. This wave of aggression by the Japanese caused the Chinese people to renew their patriotism and they fought back with a vengeance.

Japan did not expect the outcome. There was no victory for either side. The Japanese Imperial Army estimated that 100,000 soldiers had lost their lives and that 3,500,000 Chinese had been slain and fifty million more were homeless.

The Japanese were not to be discouraged nor would they allow themselves to lose face. The Emperor Jimmu Tenno, legendary founder of the oldest reigning dynasty on earth, is said to have made the following statement as a tenet to his people: "We shall build our capitol all over the world, and make the whole world our dominion."

Had the Western powers exercised their sanctions during the time of the Japanese invasion of China, they could have paralyzed the Japanese war machine. All they needed to do was to interrupt the sources of supplies being shipped to Japan or China from abroad. But both London and Washington preferred to arm their enemies. Japan regularly bought eighty percent of its arms, oil, fuel and motors from American and British companies. And just prior to the incident at Pearl Harbor, the United States had shipped over $700,000,000 worth of scrap metal, finished steel, machine tools, gasoline, copper and zinc to Japan.

The Western powers did not pay attention to what was taking place in front of them. Had they done so, history would have been changed forever. Unfortunately, America fell victim to a fact of life: those who do not familiarize themselves with history are doomed to repeat the same mistakes.

Tokyo began to test the waters, first in December of 1937 by bombing an American gunboat, the USS Panay, along with three

American oil tankers on the Yangtze River. President Roosevelt protested to Emperor Hirohito and eventually accepted an apology and compensation. Next, Japan increased its military personnel in those areas of China that it still held. It further cut off Hong Kong from all outside commerce and closed the Yangtze to foreign shipping. Japanese planes bombed British gunboats. Tokyo pressured Paris to stop arms shipments to China by threatening action against France's territory in Indo-China. Britain's Chamberlain put on airs of being upset but did not make any move to do anything more.

Timing was perfect for Japan and for the growing Nazi regime in Germany and the Fascist party in Italy. They knew that an alliance with Germany and Italy would threaten Britain and America with war on two oceans. Tokyo could see the advantage and agreed with the German-Italian alliance but stopped short of actually signing on with them. It was not until the Japanese realized the opportunities a Nazi victory over the West would present to them that they did join in a pact binding the Axis Powers together. This was called a new order in Europe and the pact linked Germany, Italy and Japan in an association that would guarantee to assist one another with all political, economic and military means. Should any one of them be attacked by any outside power, they would come to one another's defense. Japanese Ambassador Kuruso stated that the pact would "become a sword in the hand of the righteous warrior and thus contribute to the reestablishment of universal peace." America was then warned clearly to stand aside while the conquerors completed their tasks. They were further warned that if the United States refused to understand the real intentions of Japan, Germany and Italy, there would be no other course open than to go to war. America was not impressed.

Although Japan claimed a desire for peace, the United States was far more interested in deeds than statements. In England, Churchill welcomed assurances that Japan had no anti-British moves in mind but rejected any thought of mediation between London and Berlin. By threatening war as the Reich's ally, Japan had angered America and Britain. By proposing peace, it had angered Germany.

The United States would not be pushed into a corner. It was the foremost power in the world. An American loan of $25,000,000 to China was announced, followed by another of $100,000,000. As though to further emphasize its strength, American sales of scrap iron and steel and of high-test gasoline to Japanese buyers were further restricted. But Tokyo was still free to buy finished iron and steel, old ships and all forms of low grade oil products. During 1940 two million barrels of oil per month flowed across the Pacific from American refineries to supply the Japanese tanks and planes that brought death to a million Chinese; much of it was transported in American-owned tankers, transferred to Panamanian or other tankers of foreign registry. Englishmen lost battles for lack of tankers. New Englanders paid more and more for gasoline. The American oil companies were guided by the State Department, which insisted that shipments to Japan must continue otherwise Tokyo might be tempted to seize the oil fields of the Dutch Indies. The diplomatic bureaucrats in Washington hinted that serious restrictions on trade with nations

9

friendly to the Axis would be unwise; such nations could show retaliation by becoming friendly with the Axis. Americans, therefore, continued to give generous aid to China and to denounce Japanese aggression while selling to Japan the means of continuing the aggression. Nothing made sense, especially to the Chinese.

Despite their quiet satisfaction over this state of affairs, Tokyo's warlords were disturbed by other American moves. The signing of the Berlin pact produced no visible slackening of American efforts to aid Britain. Said Roosevelt: "No combination of dictator countries will stop the help we are giving. Our decision is made." Ten days after the pact was signed the State Department urged all Americans in the Far East to return home. Tokyo jumped at what looked like an anticipation of war. The Japanese Foreign Office said there was no reason to be so nervous. They wished Americans would understand that there was nothing to be alarmed about, the pact was not against the United States but for the United States – as a means of keeping America out of war. The American fleet remained in Hawaii. American bombers moved into Manila. America prepared for a two-ocean navy and called up men to serve in the army and the air force. Britain reinforced Singapore.

Five days before the ceremony of signing in Berlin, Vichy and Tokyo signed another pact. This pact allowed the establishment of three Japanese air bases in northern Indo-China. These arrangements were made as a means for a tenuous friendship between France and Japan. Access to Indo-China enabled the Japanese Army to bomb the Burma Road more easily, stopping the flow of material to their enemy. It also enabled Tokyo to secure new supplies of rice by pressuring the French authorities, and new supplies of oil by threatening the Dutch in the East Indies. In mid-November, the Dutch officials and the agents of Shell Oil and Socony Vacuum consented to quadruple sales of oil from the Netherlands Indies to Japan. Yet, even with this pact, many in Tokyo still were worried. The Chinese war went on in a hopeless and costly deadlock. New friction in China between Chiang Kai-Shek and his Communist allies stirred hopes, but such hopes also brought no peace.

As Japan played its political games with Germany and Italy, and separately with France, it also looked toward Russia to establish a relationship with the Stalinist regime. Japan would now hold a similar pact as that of Germany to Russia. Strangely enough, that which Stalin granted to Japan was something which Stalin had many times asked of Tokyo earlier and had been as many times refused: a peace pact. But Japan, whose populace depended heavily upon fish for sustenance, was now the beggar and Russia the giver. The Kremlin had driven a hard bargain in the annual renewal of the fisheries treaty. For a five year period it pledged Japan and the USSR to "maintain peaceful and friendly relations between them and mutually respect the territorial integrity and inviolability of the other contracting party. Should one of the contracting parties become the object of hostilities on the part of one or several third powers, the other contracting party will observe neutrality throughout the duration of the conflict."

Like all good players of the game of power, Japan was seeking something for nothing, or at least much for little. With China unconquered, they could not fight the Soviet Union.

At the end of April, 1941, the Japanese Foreign Office proposed exploratory peace terms to America. This was to include a parity of sea power with the English and the American fleets. The Mediterranean and North Africa should be abandoned by Britain. Gibraltar, Malta, Aden, Singapore, Hong Kong and all American bases west of Hawaii should be demilitarized. All the world should be divided into spheres. But in the American sphere, more specifically South America, the United States should grant full equality to the Axis and its allies.

Japan claimed it was very anxious to maintain friendly relations with the United States and it saw no reason why the two countries could not remain friendly. It said it considered that the German-Japanese alliance was designed to keep the United States from involvement in the European war.

The United States remained wary of Japan and on July 25 of that year, President Roosevelt ordered the freezing of all Japanese assets in the United States and, at the request of Chungking, all Chinese assets as well. That region of China was afraid that the Nanking province, which was under Japanese influence, might use those assets for assistance to Japan. General Douglas MacArthur was recalled to active service to take over the army of the Philippine Commonwealth, which was placed on war status under American command. Silk imports were stopped and oil exports were limited with a threat of full suspension. London followed suit and denounced the commercial treaties of Britain, Burma and India with Japan, at the same time reinforcing Singapore, Malaya and the road to Mandalay. The Netherlands Indies suspended the agreement by which Japan had been promised 1,800,000 tons of oil per year.

These moves caused Japanese stock prices to fall to a ten-year low. The Silk Exchange closed its doors. When Washington protested sharply at the end of the month over the bombing of the US gunboat Tutuila, anchored in Yangtze off the coast of Chungking, Tokyo apologized even though it had retaliated, measure for measure, for the economic blows struck by the American-English alliance. Unfortunately, due to the alliance's errors in years past, the Japanese army and navy had ample stocks of oil for another year. But Japan could not survive a full economic boycott. If the democracies meant business by allowing Japan no business, Japan would be ruined – unless Japan could conquer the Indies and defeat the Western Powers in war.

The United States declared war on Japan on the eighth of December, 1941, immediately after the bombing of Pearl Harbor, Hawaii on December seventh.

On the sixth of August, 1945, at 8:16 a.m., the first atomic bomb was dropped on Hiroshima killing an estimated 71,000 people. Within five years that total was to reach 200,000 based upon the fallout created by the explosion.

This bomb, which contained uranium as its primary detonation material, was called "Little Boy" and had been ten and a half feet long, twenty-four inches in diameter, and weighed 9,700 pounds. It looked like and elongated trash can with fins.

The second bomb was known as "Fat Man" and exploded at 11:02 a.m.on August 9, 1945, destroying the city of Nagasaki. The "Fat Man" was a five-foot sphere weighing two tons. Its blast caused the death of 38,000 people and within five years, its fallout resulted in the death of 100,000 more victims. Overall, Japan lost nearly two million citizens in the Second World War.

Japan surrendered to the United States at 2:00 a.m. on August 15, 1945, Tokyo time. The Imperial Majesty of Japan had stated "We declared war on America and Britain out of our sincere desire to ensure Japan's self-preservation and the stabilization of Southeast Asia. It being far from our thought to infringe upon the sovereignty of other nations or to embark upon territorial aggrandizement."

He did not say that Japan lost the war; that was perhaps to soften the humiliation of his subjects. He did not think of it as a surrender at all, but only as a truce in the unfinished war for international equality, which his nation had begun with the treaties forced upon his great-grandfather by Commodore Perry and Consul Harris some ninety years before.

Ideals die hard, and hatred reigns.

There are no national leaders who have found any way to achieve material progress without imposing hardships upon their own people and arousing the fear and antagonism of other nations. In any country, power and happiness are always incompatible.

"Power and liberty are like heat and moisture; where they are well mixed, everything prospers; where they are single, they are destructive."   Saville

CHAPTER TWO – ITALY

"I passed by his garden, and marked, with one eye, how the Owl and the Panther were sharing a pie: the Panther took pie-crust, and gravy, and meat, while the Owl had the dish as its share of the treat. When the pie was all finished, the Owl, as a boon, was kindly permitted to pocket the spoon: while the Panther received knife and fork with a growl, and concluded the banquet by... "[1]

* * * * *

It is not an easy thing to be poor. Still, poverty is bearable if only one has a place he can be sure of. What is worse is to be treated as an outcast, to have one's self-respect destroyed, to be alone and afraid and friendless in a world, which is brutal or condescending. For men, and for nations of men, this can and often does break one's spirit. Some become helpless, resigned, without will. I know, I can have empathy for anyone who has suffered being poor. Permit me to explain. In my earlier years, I was employed by Sears as their eastern property manager for new site construction. All my life I had enjoyed the privilege of having and creating a comfortable income. However, there had been a period of time when I, too, discovered a lifestyle far from what I had been used to, and adjusting to it was very difficult.

In 1980, after having lived in some very affluent surroundings, my wife and I moved to Connecticut from where I originally had begun my working career. I had just completed an endeavor in Rockport, Maine, where I purchased the Samoset Resort and had been renovating it after its closure some years previously. Unfortunately, vandals had struck the property and it burned to the ground. In my efforts to construct a new resort, I became involved with a financial institution, which financed the new resort hotel and who put on a wonderful appearance as an REIT, a real estate investment trust. However, the company turned out to have their own agenda. They wanted the hotel property and acquired it by refusing to fund the balance of the loan. Why not? The hotel had two-hundred acres of pristine land and a half-mile of ocean frontage and was now ready to be opened for business. In a true sense, they stole it. As a result, I lost all my assets and was cast the responsibility of paying additional debt that forced me to file for bankruptcy. My purpose in going to Connecticut was two-fold. First, to gain a new start in life in an area that I was familiar with; and second, to struggle to regain my footing in the business world. At that time, my wife and I were broke. This was the lowest point in my life. I was lost not knowing where to turn or what to do. I saw no future and I even asked God to take me. Our home in Connecticut was up for foreclosure and the property had a sign to that effect posted in the front yard. I had given a local real estate broker the listing in an effort to beat out the foreclosure.

Where others in my position might have gone through with something as drastic as what I had considered, I was blessed by a miracle. Within two months, a buyer came along. A man from Washington, DC made an offer to pay not only what I was asking for the place but enough to cover all my outstanding debt. The attorney at the closing had never seen anything like this before in his career. I

17

never met the man who bought the house and never was able to find out his name. As I said it was an absolute miracle.

Others have not been so lucky. Many are consumed by a fierce thirst for vengeance, for violent self-assertion, for power over those who are callous or contemptuous. Power to command obedience, power to inspire fear, power to deprive others of all dignity – this brings peace of soul. Men escape fear by acting like beasts in order that they may feel like gods. So it was for Benito Mussolini, born July 29, 1883, in the village of Dovia di Predappio near Forli, living in a poor province of a poor land.

At the age of nine he was sent to a school run by the Salesian Fathers at Faenza. Here he was exposed to ridicule, a result of the third-class status, which his own poverty and the snobbery of others imposed upon him. After two stormy years he got himself expelled. Later he went to normal school and eventually secured a license as an elementary school teacher.

This hopeful young man, like millions of others, became the victim of those with wealth and power who would not or could not agree with his methods of teaching, which allowed for students to exercise their individuality. Later he found it necessary to reassert his importance by coercing and repressing his pupils in a larger school. Between the generous teacher and the power-driven tyrant lay years of anguish and turmoil.

Teaching left him dissatisfied. He could not accede to the overbearance of the rich and powerful so he left his job. He moved to Switzerland to evade military service where he begged and starved. In

Lausanne he was arrested for vagrancy. He found contentment only when he became a labor organizer and a social orator and journalist. He was arrested and expelled from Bern. The police began to watch him as a dangerous radical labeled as a violent character. In Geneva he became *Duce*, or leader, of the local Italian Socialist Club. Here, too, the authorities expelled him. He preached Marxism; wrote inflammatory articles; harangued the crowd; mingled with international firebrands; and eventually returned to Italy late in 1904 to do the military service that he had previously avoided.

His two years in Switzerland fixed the pattern of his life. In a society which he feared and hated, he found reassurance only by winning the public accolades of others as discontented as himself. In his private life he made no friends and found no peace. He pursued women, made love, begot illegitimate children, but all without joy or tenderness. By 1910 he was living with Rachele Guidi, a quiet woman whom he met when she was working in a small tavern, which had at one time been owned by his father.

Their first child was a girl whom they named Edda. Not until the coming of the Great War did he marry Rachele. Other women came and went but his only grand passion was for rebellion. His one true love was a love for the applause of rebels and for the power which command over mobs can give.

In 1910, he founded a paper called *The Class Struggle*. He played Socialist politics as an uncompromising extremist. He opposed all cooperation with the middle-class, property-owning people. He attacked the Republicans so viciously that the local paper responded by calling him vulgar, indecent, nauseating, insensitive, a vagabond in the pay of Jewish societies, pretentious, conscienceless, paranoiac, a ferocious madman, a rancorous inciter, an unscrupulous liar, a most vile and delinquent sower of hatred, a trickster, a hack-writer, a maniac, an imbecile, and a disgusting reptile.

By 1912, he was a national leader of the Socialists. He held that God was a fraud, the Pope a charlatan, the King a fake, the ruling classes a set of thieves, and national flag a rag to be planted on a dunghill. He was all fury and violence. Yet, he differed from other fanatics. His insatiable thirst for power proved more potent than his attachment to the cause through which his thirst had first begun. When war broke out in 1914, with Italy neutral, he first supported the Socialist position of uncompromising opposition to intervention. But by October he was asking the Executive of the Party to declare against unconditional neutrality. All were against him.

Mussolini joined the army in November, 1915. He saw little service in the face of the enemy even though he suffered a battle wound that took him away from the front.

Italy's only military asset was its population, but Italians were the lest warlike of peoples. Numbers count for little without iron, coal, capital, control of seaways and possession of bases – and in these things Italy was poor. Italy emerged from the war and the subsequent peace impoverished and divided against itself by a bitter class struggle. The Socialist leaders who now won a huge following vied with the Communists among their ranks by preaching revolution to the poor. Land-owners and businessmen were terrified into a frantic search for a savior. Democrats were paralyzed. Even the Populist Party of Catholic liberals seemed to offer no hope to the insecure. Strikes and riots swept the land. The disgruntled war veterans, jobless, desperate and restless after plunging from the excitement of battle and victory into the miseries of a shameful peace, became a fertile field for political scoundrels and idealists, for reformers, rebels and demagogues. They formed various leagues, societies and *fasci,* or groups, of the discontented under rival leaders who preached a dozen fanatic gospels of salvation.

One such group, calling itself the *Fasci di Combattimento,* was established in Milan on March 23, 1919, under the leadership of Benito Mussolini. Its program was democratic, patriotic, republican, socialistic, anti-imperialist, and pro-League of Nations. Its *duce* demanded land for the peasants and bullets for profiteers. The Socialist Party denounced him as a turncoat and he denounced the Socialists as lukewarm opportunists and betrayers of the workers. Only he could lead the revolution. In the election campaign of November, 1919, the *Fascisti* championed universal suffrage, votes for women, minimum wages, and eight-hour day, workers participation in industry, social insurance, nationalization of the arms industry, anti-clericalism, a pacific foreign policy and a capital levy. But no Fascist candidates were successful. In Milan, Mussolini got 5,000 votes out of 346,000.

In 1920 came more strikes and riots, the lockout of the metal workers and finally widespread seizure of factories by revolutionaries. The propertied classes were panic-stricken at the government's inaction. Mussolini seized his chance and promised to destroy the Socialist Party. Money flowed from the well-to-do to the Fascist coffers. By the spring of 1921 the Fasciti were 100,000 strong. They elected 35 members to parliament, including their leader. They formed military gangs or squads to beat up or murder Socialists, to wreck and burn the headquarters of trade unions, cooperatives and leftist newspapers. Army officers joined with them. The police remained neutral.

Mussolini, now a member of a hopelessly divided parliament, urged an end to the murder and arson. He was concerned a civil war might break out before he was ready for victory. But his fiery followers had tasted blood and wanted more.

Patriots were persuaded that the Duce would save the state. Priests were convinced that he would save the church. Plutocrats and aristocrats were certain that he would save property. All were deceived by their own illusions.

Those no longer capable of governing themselves must be governed by others. Those unable to act together to preserve their freedom must separately and contemptibly lose their birthright. The result of the weakness of freedom is tyranny – a form of governance which men seldom prefer to liberty, but always prefer to anarchy.

The Duce's first task was to militarize his countrymen by preaching the message of "Believe, Obey, Fight" and by instilling faith in the glory of the fatherland. Rome's ancient grandeur was to be restored. Mussolini was to be imperator and conqueror. Italy was to be made formidable and, therefore, respected. Every phase of life was to be mobilized to the supreme end of the power of the nation. In the name of national solidarity, the old trade unions were dissolved and the right to strike suppressed. In the name of unity and power, the youth were imbued with tribal mysticism. The tyranny was rationalized and sanctified. The state concluded its long struggle with the Papacy through the Treaty and Concordat of 1929 in which it restored the temporal authority of the Pope and recognized Vatican City as a sovereign territory. The Republican who made peace with the King was the atheist who made peace with the Pope. Principles were nothing; power was all.

Mussolini wanted more. Italy could afford to use violence only against small and feeble states. When an Italian general was assassinated by Greek patriots near the Albanian border, Mussolini ordered the bombardment and seizure of the island of Corfu and defied the League of Nations to stop him. The victory was glorious: fifteen orphan children were killed by the shells. An indemnity and apology were extracted from Greece, but under pressure, Corfu was evacuated and Rome gained no conquests.

Mussolini was still impelled by the slow impoverishment of the masses under Fascism to counteract popular unrest by fulfilling long-deferred promises of war and glory. The Nazi revolution in Germany gave him his chance. He sponsored the futile Four Power Pact of 1933 in which Rome, Paris, London and Berlin agreed to consult one another to promote peace and disarmament. A month later he met Hitler for the first time in Venice, but the two tyrants could come to no agreement.

Hitler was a strategist. He knew history and he knew the right buttons to push to gather his people behind him. Mussolini was a buffoon. Every move he made was influenced by his passion. And every move he made was foolish and wrong if it was to be of any benefit to Italy.

In 1932, Mussolini had planned an invasion of Ethiopia in Africa. He perceived from the fate of Manchuria that Britain and France, despite their pledges to enforce peace, would do nothing against aggression where their own interests were not directly endangered. Yet he feared that their leaders might regard an attack on Ethiopia as a threat to their own African colonies. And Italy was too weak to risk a clash with the democratic powers.

His solution was to sell them Italian support against Germany – and Italian sponsorship of the independence of Austria, which had fallen under German influence – in return for their support of his African ambitions.

Pierre Laval, Foreign Minister of France, feared Communism. He admired Fascism. He could see only one means to make France secure against Germany: an alliance with Italy. He could see only one means of making Fascist Italy a strong and willing ally: cooperation in Mussolini's African designs. To buy Italian friendship at the expense of a remote kingdom of barbarians seemed cheap and easy.

The result was the signature of elaborate accords, pledging peace, friendship and consultation. Laval got no alliance but only a vague promise to consult in case of any threat to Austrian independence or any danger of Nazi repudiation of disarmament obligations. He consented to collaboration in developing African colonies and to Italian participation.

Mussolini was determined to invade Ethiopia without any pretext. In one conversation he was heard to have said, "If you offered me all of Ethiopia on a silver platter, I would refuse it, for I have resolved to take it by force."

Laval and the British Foreign Minister, Sir Samuel Hoare, reluctantly concluded that Mussolini would attack and that they must make a pretense at Geneva of imposing sanctions. Otherwise the voters of Britain and France, convinced that their own safety lay in support of the League of Nations and enforcement of the covenant against aggressors, might turn them out of office and elect honest men in their places.

In the name of peace, the French and English leaders told their countrymen that sanctions must be kept innocuous so that Europe would not be plunged into bloodshed. Laval consented to weak sanctions but Hoare disagreed when his French friends, recalling that Hitler had repudiated the military clauses of Versailles, asked a promise of sanctions against Germany in the event of further treaty-breaking. London and Paris assured Rome that sanctions would be purely economic and would not interrupt the Fascist program. Rome assured Laval and Hoare that Italy would not retaliate with force but would remain on the defensive. Hoare assured Hitler that Britain would not join France in any future sanctions against the Reich. Hitler assured Hoare that Germany would not join Italy or move against France during the crisis.

On October 1, 1935, Mussolini ordered the invasion of Ethiopia. Rome informed the League that Ethiopian mobilization was a threat, aggravated by the withdrawal of Ethiopian troops from the border, and that the warlike and aggressive spirit of Ethiopia has succeeded in imposing war against Italy.

Ethiopia had appealed to the League of Nations for assistance, but the League, convinced by members that Italy had gone to war in an effort to produce peace, abandoned Ethiopia.

Haile Selassie, the King of Ethiopia told the League, "The Ethiopian people, to whom all assistance was refused, are climbing alone their path to Calvary. No humiliation has been spared the victim of aggression. Many threatened powers have uttered the cry of panic and rout: 'Everyone for himself.' It is a certainty that they would be abandoned, as Ethiopia has been, and between two evils they have chosen one which the fear of aggression led them to consider the lesser. May God forgive them. There are different ways to maintain peace. There is maintenance of peace through right and there is peace at any price. The League would be committing suicide if after having been created to maintain peace through right it were to abandon that principle and adopt instead the principle of peace at any price, even the price of immolation of a member state at the feet of its aggressors."

The Council chose suicide. Council President Wilhelm Munters of Latvia declared that each member should decide for itself whether to recognize Italian title to Ethiopia. Only four delegations objected: New Zealand, Bolivia, China and the USSR. Britain and

France recognized Italian title to Ethiopia in November. Seventeen months later Mussolini reciprocated with a declaration of war against those who had sought to buy peace by giving him an empire.

With the aid of his French and English friends the Duce destroyed the League of Nations, humiliated Britain and rendered France ripe for defeat at the hands of the Reich. He also conquered a kingdom. In the winning of it much easy glory went to Mussolini and to the members of his family.

In May, 1936, Mussolini addressed the people of Italy telling them, "Today, May 5, at 4 p.m., at the head of the victorious troops, I entered Addis Ababa. Ethiopia is Italian. It is Italian in fact because it is occupied by our victorious armies. It is Italian in law because of the law of Rome and civilization which triumphs over barbarism, justice which triumphs over cruel whims, redemption of miseries which triumph over slavery."

Italy now had a greater reputation. With its enhanced prestige in the Mediterranean, it realized more opportunities in other directions. The Sudan and the headwaters of the Nile lay adjacent to Italian Ethiopia. The British route to India through the Red Sea was apparently at the mercy of Italy. French communications with North Africa might be severed by Italian air power, particularly in the event of cooperation from a Fascist Spain. Intrigues against Britain and France throughout the Arab world offered hope of further weakening the influence of London and Paris in the Near East. Mussolini was driven forward to continued aggression designed to give the masses circuses instead of bread.

Mussolini now turned his eyes toward Spain. Controlling the coasts of Spain would enable the Axis Powers to levy further blackmail against France and Britain and perhaps ultimately to destroy them. The Axis crusade could be disguised in terms, which would lead the rest of the world to believe that it was going forward in order to save Spain from Communism. Mussolini and Hitler assumed correctly that most men of property and strong religious faith in France, Britain and America would be easily deceived by the purpose of this crusade and would either acquiesce or cooperate in the destruction of the Spanish Republic.

Spain's military leader, General Francisco Franco, was open to assistance from Mussolini and Hitler to quell a civil war that had triggered in Spain between the elected People's Front Cabinet and the ousted monarchist leaders. The People's Front was neither Socialist nor Communist, but the perception given by Mussolini and Hitler to the world was otherwise.

With little effort and with Britain, France and the United States remaining out of the conflict with Spain and showing further neutrality by refusing to sell arms to Spain, Italy and Germany, backed by Franco and his followers, began the takeover of Spain.

Nearly 100,000 Italian troops entered the country. Barcelona, the new capitol of Spain and the office for the People's Front Cabinet, was bombed by the Axis Powers, killing 245 women and 118 children among its victims.

Franco now had Spain under his control. But did Franco realize he was under the control of Mussolini and Hitler?

Mussolini, in his arrogance, and based upon intelligence he had received, decided that France was doomed and that Britain would soon be crushed. As far as France was concerned, he was correct, however Britain would prove to be tough.

On September 27, 1940, Mussolini joined the Triple Alliance of Germany and Japan. He followed that up by proposing to invade British Somaliland, Kenya, the Sudan, Egypt and Greece. Only the first of these invasions attained its objective. On October 29, Hitler met with Mussolini while the Italian army in Albania launched an invasion of Greece. However, the Greek dictator, John Metaxas, who had studied war and politics in Germany, threw back the Italian army in a stand-off. The Italians then headed to Albania and centered their aggressions there. British air and sea forces now had access to Greek bases and used them to raid Naples, smash Italian battleships at Taranto, bomb Valona and Durazzo and interrupt communications across the Straits of Otranto. The Greeks, having been challenged by the failed Italian army, now went on to attack the Italians and retake three cities where the Italian army had been stationed. Britain's military forces launched a battle at the Nile and retook Sidi Barrani, invaded Libya, captured Bardia, and went on to Tobruk and Bengazi. They seized 150,000 prisoners along with huge stores at a cost of 438 lives and 1249 wounded.

Suddenly, the power of Italy was being brought to the brink of disaster. Mussolini lost all of his East African empire. Before much more was lost, he was forced to turn to the German Reich for help. Germany had to rescue him and with that rescue came the ownership of all of Italy and its holdings by Hitler. Italy was lost and Mussolini, who had deluded the masses for a number of years, no longer had a cause or a fatherland.

At the same time that Mussolini was holding the reigns of power in Italy as a puppet leader, Hitler was organizing an agreement with the Vatican in Rome. In later years it was to be called Hitler's Pope and the signing of the Reich Concordat. This was a treaty made between the Catholic Church leaders and Hitler in which the Church accepted an obligation under the terms of this agreement that imposed a moral duty on all Catholics to obey the Nazi rulers. It was signed on September10, 1933 by Eugenio Pacelli, Pope Pius XII. This Pope reigned from 1939 to 1958 and was hailed as a brilliant Vatican lawyer who had negotiated the treaty with Hitler. The Reich Concordat was to ensure that the Nazis would rise unopposed. This would, of course, seal the fate of all Jews in Europe. There was, however, a major problem because of the fact that a number of Jews had converted to Catholicism and the Third Reich was requested to offer protection to them under the Concordat as well. This was a problem that was never resolved.

Italy, as well as Germany, surrendered on May 7, 1945. All military operations ceased at 11:01 p.m. on May 8, 1945. Churchill had pressed for a May 7 date for the official surrender; Truman wanted May 8, as that was his 61st birthday; and Stalin wanted May 9th. The final decision was determined as May 8 at 9:00 a.m. Washington time. This was called V-E Day for Victory in Europe.

As Harry Truman stated in April of 1958, "A politician is a man who understands government, and it takes a politician to run a government. A statesman is a politician who's been dead ten to fifteen years." Harry Truman got his way with Churchill and Stalin.

Harry Truman had been President of the United States two days less than four weeks. The fighting across Europe had lasted six years, ten months and sixteen days. The total number of troops that were engaged in the war was estimated at nine million. The deaths of American soldiers totaled 135,576.

Truman's euphoric V-E Day statement, which quoted "The flags of freedom fly all over Europe" would prove to be premature.

CHAPTER THREE – GERMANY

*"The Walrus and the Carpenter were walking close at hand:
They wept like anything to see such quantities of sand. 'If this were
only cleared away,' they said 'it would be grand!' 'O Oysters, come
and walk with us!' the Walrus did beseech. 'A pleasant walk, a
pleasant talk, along the briny beach: we cannot do with more than
four, to give a hand to each.' And four young oysters hurried up, all
eager for the treat. Their coats were brushed, their faces washed,
their shoes were clean and neat – And this was odd, because, you
know, they hadn't any feet. Four other oysters followed them, and yet
another four; and thick and fast they came at last, and more, and
more, and more – All hopping through the frothy waves, and
scrambling to the shore. 'A loaf of bread,' the Walrus said, 'is what
we chiefly need. Pepper and vinegar besides are very good indeed –
Now, if you're ready, Oysters dear, we can begin to feed.' 'But not
on us!' the Oysters cried, turning a little blue. 'After such kindness,
that would be a dismal thing to do!' 'The night is fine,' the Walrus
said, 'Do you admire the view?' 'I weep for you,' the Walrus said. 'I
deeply sympathize.' With sobs and tears he sorted out those of the
largest size, holding his pocket-handkerchief before his streaming
eyes. 'O Oysters,' said the Carpenter, 'you've had a pleasant run!
Shall we be trotting home again?' But answer came there none. And
this was scarcely odd, because they'd eaten every one."* [1]

* * * * *

Karl der Grosse was the first leader to organize Germany
under what was known as the First Reich. It was formed early in the
first millennium when the Germanic tribes had long since learned to
revere and imitate the great world of ancient Rome, which their
ancestors had destroyed. For centuries, a unique coalition existed in
which medieval Christians linked by the common culture of

Frenchmen, Germans, Czechs, poles, Italians and others were bound together by the Church and the ruling emperors. It remained such until the late 1800's when the Second Reich was formed as nationalism and Christianity, including the movement of Protestantism, became the encouraging force. However, during those years, a new leader was emerging who wanted to return to the disgraceful cult of imperial power, one that practiced barbarism and paganism. Adolf Hitler dreamed of a world state in which he was the ruler and his subjects were loyal only to him. This would be accomplished by the might of the sword and would be known as the Third Reich.

To the people of Germany in the twentieth century, this leader was a holy man and a redeemer, sent by the Teutonic gods to save Germany and the world from the Jews and the Communists. To most of the other people of the world, he was a diabolical degenerate and the scourge of God. On the day on which he began the greatest of his aggressions, Britain's Winston Churchill described him as "a monster of wickedness, insatiable in his lust for blood and plunder."

Hitler, like Mussolini and Stalin, became a leader of people like himself; people who were frightened, terrified of their own loneliness in a harsh and ill-ordered world that denied them security and love. Like all geniuses, he was more talented than most of the populace. Like all politicians, he was in need of public acclaim to bring comfort to his twisted mind. He was a little man, transformed by his own magic and by the paranoid delusions of his followers into a savior with a sword. His father was a shoemaker named Alois

Schicklgruber, the illegitimate son of Maria Schicklgruber. She married the boy's father when Alois was five. Not till the boy was a man of forty did he change his name to Hitler, after the Austrian peasant family from which his father came.

Alois Hitler was helped by his first wife to secure a post in the Austrian customs service. His second wife died within a year after their marriage. His third wife was a distant cousin who had been a maid in his first wife's home and it was this wife who gave birth to the son they would call Adolf.

When the son was seven, his father retired on a pension. When the son was almost fourteen, his father died. Three years later his mother died. Adolf had hated his father and quarreled with his mother. They wanted him to become a respectable official. He wanted to be an artist. Now he was free. But he was alone and poor. He went to Vienna to study art. He failed. Having no money, he worked as a building trades laborer and learned, out of his poverty and bitterness, to hate Social Democrats and Jews and Slavs. Since no one loved him, he loved no one. In his early twenties he painted postcards and lived in misery, first in Vienna and then in Munich. His hero fantasies came true in 1914. War brought meaning to an otherwise empty life. He joined the German forces, tasted mud and blood, became a corporal and was given the honorable Iron Cross.

There was no way Adolf Hitler could go back to civilian life. He remained with the army after the war and watched with loathing the rise and bloody fall of the Bavarian Soviet Republic. Marxists and Jews seemed to him more than ever the enemies of the mystical fatherland, which he worshipped with all the devotion of a repressed romanticist incapable of normal passion. He shunned women and lectured the members of his regiment on the duties of patriotism. Where Munich was full of riff-raff, Revolutionaries, reactionaries, political revivalists and all types of salvationists, Hitler attended meetings looking for an outlet to the hatreds he harbored and a means of expressing his ambitions.

On one evening in 1919, he came upon a meeting of anti-Semitic fanatics calling themselves the German Labor Party. Hitler was impressed by what he witnessed and joined the party. He took his duties seriously and discovered his talent as an orator. His expounding in beer-halls of his bitter denunciation of the Jews, the Marxists and the Allies brought crowds in to listen to him. He persuaded his fellow soldiers to join the party. That was an easy enticement as most of the existing members were disgruntled war veterans. By spring, Hitler was the leader of the group, now named the National Socialist German Workers Party.

Every week Hitler harangued the crowds, damning Jews and Masons, capitalists and Communists, democrats and monarchists with impartial fury and preaching the liberation of Germany from those he deemed were holding it in slavery. Every week more members and more money flowed to the party.

Hitler found that symbols, songs and pageantry won converts. The heated oratory of hatred fired them with fanaticism. Other trouble-makers and adventurers joined the cause: Hermann Goring, wealthy war ace and dope addict; Rudolf Hess, soldier and anti-

Semite; Ernest Rohm, war veteran, terrorist and homosexual; Edmund Heines, patriotic murderer; Gregor Strasser, soldier and druggist; Alfred Rosenberg, Baltic German and rabid anti-Bolshevik; General Erick von Ludendorff, ex-warlord and political lunatic; and thousand of smaller misfits.

By the autumn of 1923, the party had 70,000 members. Like Mussolini's movement, it had support from the wealthy and influential who hoped to use it for their own ends. With this support, Hitler planned his revolution for the anniversary of the Jewish-Marxist revolt, which ousted the Kaiser.

Even though Hitler's move was opportune, this first revolt was met with great opposition and with poor commitment from those within his party. It failed and Hitler was arrested. During his stay in prison, he wrote *Mein Kampf*, my struggle.

The status of Germany's power was weak. The financial condition of the German government led to huge budgetary deficits, which were met with inflation, with a resulting depreciation of the mark. In January of 1923, months before Hitler's revolution, French and Belgian troops seized Dusseldorf, Essen and other mining and smelting centers in the Ruhr valley. Germany countered by stopping all reparation payments being made from previous conflicts, and organizing passive resistance against the invaders. The forces of occupation resorted to reprisals, arrests, courts-martial, and other repressive measures. But coal could not be mined with bayonets and the occupation was fruitless. The German government, as a result of all this, was reduced to bankruptcy. Only the false prosperity of the

1920's, nourished by American and British loans, enabled Germany's Weimar Republic to survive as long as it did.

When the Great Depression descended upon the Reich, paralyzing the money markets, halting the wheels of heavy industry, bankrupting the insecure middle class, and depriving millions of workers of their jobs, the enemies of the Republic for the first time found a mass following. Conservatives and liberals were spurned by the desperate masses. Armies of converts flocked to the sides of the reactionaries and radicals. Hungry laborers joined the Communist cause. Frightened peasants looked to the extreme right for protection. Aristocrats and plutocrats conspired to feather their nests.

In every corner of the land the agitators whose shrieking was shrillest, whose cursing was the most colorful and whose promises were the most extravagant were the preachers of National Socialism. They cried that Germany was undefeated in 1918 but was stabbed in the back by the Jews and the Marxists; that the criminals of the Weimar Jew Republic must be destroyed; that the Reich could recover freedom and bread through a new messiah who would save all souls and fill all stomachs in a glorious Third Reich. That messiah, wearing a tan raincoat and a battered hat, flew like a madman from town to town. At a thousand meetings he climaxed a grand drama of pageantry and music with the hoarse eloquence of hysteria, arms waving, hair flying, sweat streaming, voice screaming, choking and thundering in fury. Under his spell millions found their souls by losing their minds. Their savior was Adolf Hitler.

During this period of time, the United States was running into some problems of its own, not the least of which was the devastation of the Great Depression. The state of the economy touched every class from the wealthiest, who had suffered enormous losses in the stock market, to the poorest, who scratched for every penny. Many of the poor had been in the military during World War I and that had provided them with a regular paycheck every month. With the war having ended, so did that guarantee of a set income. However, the veterans of World War I had been promised by the government certain bonuses in the form of cash. When nothing transpired, a contingent of them marched on Washington DC in 1932 seeking what they had been assured back in 1924 but had never received. It was compensation that would amount to one dollar a day for domestic military service and one dollar and twenty-five cents a day for each day spent overseas.

Legislation was passed years earlier, which culminated in the presentation of certificates to each soldier reflecting the amount due to him, and to be redeemed in1945. This legislation was vetoed by President Calvin Coolidge who declared that "patriotism which is bought and paid for is not patriotism."

In 1929, Congressman Wright Patman of Texas sponsored a bill asking for the immediate cash payment of this bonus money. Unfortunately, the bill never made it out of committee. In 1932, Patman resurrected the legislative bill and again tried to get it voted upon in the affirmative. In March of that year, a jobless former army sergeant named Walter Waters stood up at a veterans meeting in

Portland, Oregon and suggested that every man who had been involved in military service during WWI to hop a freight train and head to Washington to get the money that was rightfully theirs. Sorrowfully, he had no takers that day.

By May 11, a new version of Patman's bill was brought before committee but was shelved in the House of Representatives. It had attracted a critical mass of followers.

In 1932 another problem had loomed in America. Nearly 32,000 businesses failed. Unemployment soared to twenty-five percent leaving one family in four without a breadwinner. Two million people wandered the country in a futile quest for work. Many of the homeless settled in makeshift shacks called Hoovervilles after the President they blamed for their plight.

The march on Washington was a spontaneous movement of protest from every one of the forty-eight states. As the veterans headed to the country's capital, US Army intelligence reported to the White House that the Communist Party had infiltrated the veterans groups and had made a determination to overthrow the United States Government. The President did not take the report seriously and called the protest a 'temporary disease.'

The Army Deputy Chief of Staff urged the Army Chief of Staff to send the troops in to stop this group of men now being called the 'Bonus Army.' The Chief of Staff, Douglas MacArthur, dismissed the request on the grounds that this was a political, and not a military, matter. MacArthur's principle aide was Major Dwight D. Eisenhower.

The Bonus Army encamped in Washington and remained very orderly. President Hoover's Press Secretary called the marchers by a new name. He said they were no longer bonus seekers but Communists or bums. At the same time, J. Edgar Hoover was at the Justice Department trying to establish some guidance concerning Communist roots. The charge that the men had Communist roots did not have any historical substantiation.

On orders from the President, General Douglas MacArthur secretly trained his troops in riot control. What happened next is recorded in the memory of the Americans who witnessed what had transpired. For the first time in history, tanks rolled through the streets of the capital. MacArthur ordered his troops to clear the downtown area of the veterans, estimated to be about 8,000 in number. The soldiers, with the cavalry, marching with sabers drawn and pennants flying, and with George S. Patton at the head, followed by five tanks and about 300 helmeted infantrymen carrying loaded rifles and bayonets affixed to their barrels, drove the bonus army along with their wives and children, as well as pedestrians, onlookers and civil servants off the streets.

Infantrymen, wearing gas masks, hurled hundreds of tear gas grenades into the crowd. The grenades set off dozens of fires and by nightfall the entire area of downtown was evacuated.

In movie theaters across America, the scenes were shown with the army being booed and with MacArthur being jeered.

Democratic presidential nominee, Franklin D. Roosevelt, who had opposed immediate payment of the bonus army, suddenly stated to his advisor, "This will elect me."

In March of 1933, several months into FDR's first term, the bonus army marchers drifted back into Washington DC. The army set up an abandoned fort in the outskirts of Washington in which to meet. At that place, the First Lady, Eleanor Roosevelt braved mud and rain to join the veterans in a sing-a-long. The local newspaper stated, "Hoover sent the army, Roosevelt sent his wife." At that time, the President had just completed setting up the Civilian Conservation Corps known as the CCC to, at least, give the veterans a chance to work and earn some money...one dollar a day.

In June, 1936, the first veterans began cashing checks that averaged $580.00 per man. Ultimately, nearly two-billion dollars was distributed to three million World War I veterans.

At about the same time, a group of American men of wealth financed some rightist organizations not dissimilar to those in Europe and Japan. One such group prepared to initiate a *coup d'etat* by means of a private army of American Legion Veterans. Their purpose was to back General Smedley Butler for the American Presidency. This man had put down insurrections in countries whose economics were dominated by his investors. The conspirators second choice was General Douglas MacArthur. Butler, whose conscious got the best of him, exposed the plot. In subsequent testimony, Butler explained why he had been chosen as the American 'Fuhrer': "I was a high-class racketeer for capitalism." The target of the conspirators was Roosevelt's New Deal, which was being confused with Communism.

Investigation by a Congressional committee implicated the founders and leaders of the American Legion, the Governor of Massachusetts, several wealthy Wall Street brokers and high executives of Guaranty Trust, Anaconda Copper, Goodyear, Bethlehem Steel, Dupont and Remington Firearms. The sad fact is that most Americans never learned the real story. The most damaging testimony against America's fascists was suppressed. Most major newspapers refused to print the story. Many of these wealthy American businessmen proclaimed to be Christians. They were also the backers of a quasi-religious international organization called Moral Rearmament founded by a Dr. Frank Buckman, who stated, "I thank God for a man like Adolf Hitler." Buckmanism, the new religion of big business, was eventually introduced into Japan by that nation's biggest business family...the Mitsui.

With banners, drums, and trumpets, the brown-shirted Nazi storm-troopers, subsidized by businessmen and aristocrats, carried the flag throughout Germany and shouted their battle cries: "Freedon and bread!" "Out with the Jews!" and "Break the bonds of interest slavery!" In the Reichstag election of September, 1930, they won 6,400,000 votes. In the presidential election of April, 1932, 13,400,000 votes were cast for Hitler. In the Reichstag election of July, 1932, 13,745,000 votes were cast for the Nazi party. Hitler seemed about to be swept into power by a great mass movement, which would give him a majority of the electorate. But, business conditions improved slightly in the autumn of 1932 and in the last free election in Germany, the polls were down for the Nazi party. They received less than one-third of the total votes cast. By the end of the year, their movement was bankrupt and disintegrating.

The Reich did not win an electoral victory but, instead, gained its success through conspiracy. One of the former chancellors to Germany wanted back his position. He knew what power Hitler was amassing through his mob hypnotism and he decided to take advantage of that power by having Hitler working on his side. The idea was workable, the problem was that the recently elected president, Hindenburg, saw a benefit in having Hitler as the chancellor. As such, Hitler dissolved the existing Reichstag and ordered a new election, scheduled for March 5, 1933. Six days before the balloting, the Reichstag building was burned. Hitler at once accused the Communists of arson and bloody revolution. He posed as the savior of the nation from the Red menace. He ordered the arrest of thousands of Communists and Social Democrats, suppressed the campaign activities of the anti-Nazi parties, induced Hindenburg to abolish civil liberties in the name of defense against the Communist peril, and threw the electorate into a panic. His followers polled forty-four percent of the vote and secured a majority in the new Reichstag by excluding and arresting all the Communist deputies. Hitler astutely tricked his non-Nazi colleagues, wiped out all other parties, suppressed the social radicals in his own ranks, and established the Nazi despotism. The multitudes were exalted by the mass pageantry of great festivals, by the masterly propaganda of those in the party's higher levels and by the way the party appealed to the emotions of the people. Hitler was truly in control. One of the first things he did was to put to death all those who failed him in his first attempt to take the reigns of the government just prior to his arrest in 1923.

With Hindenburg's death in August of 1934, Hitler assumed the power of the presidency and took absolute power of Germany. And with the trade unions abolished and strikes forbidden, with the press, radio, motion pictures, theater, and school system shackled, and with all social organizations coordinated under Nazi control, the dictatorship was totally unlimited. Germany became devoted to fascist totalitarianism, dedicated to militarism, revenge, and imperial expansion.

The Third Reich pursued all the same general diplomatic objectives as the Weimar Republic but utilized in place of conciliation and compromise the methods of treaty-breaking, threats, and defiance. To these old objectives were added new ones far more alarming to Germany's neighbors. The Nazi youth began singing a song: "Today we have conquered Germany, tomorrow the world is ours."

The Nazi leaders fully realized that war was imminent. Any war never begins unless the aggressive force fully believes that they have a chance of victory. Hitler's problem was one of building up an overwhelming military force, dividing and weakening his prospective enemies, and finding allies. Rearmament was dangerous because it involved treaty violations and might precipitate a preventive war by the French before the Reich was prepared to resist. Hitler was cautious in his moves, calculating that French pacifism and British bewilderment would prevent any concerted effort to coerce Germany. Hitler continued to play games with the allies by making promises he had no intention of keeping. Appearances can sometimes be deceiving, especially if the aggressor purposely works to that end.

Hitler managed to increase his naval forces by breaking the treaty it had with England while it made an offer to limit its fleet to thirty-five percent of what Britain had. This was acceptable to Britain as it was led to believe that this would keep the peace.

There were several advantages to Germany: first, it allowed the build-up of its navy; second, it reduced unemployment in Germany; and third, it gave greater profits to the munitions industry as the government loans financed an enormous production of guns, tanks, artillery, bombers, submarines and battleships.

Hitler furthered his stance by proposing agreements that would give protection to the western frontier and leave Germany easy access to the east. Even though some of the members of the League of Nations did not agree with these moves and protested with warnings and condemnation, all these threats were followed by inaction. Britain pledged support to France against any German invasion but pledged nothing to Eastern Europe where conflict would obviously come first. And, although German strategists perfected a new plan to destroy France by going through Holland and Belgium, Hitler's professed objective was to keep the peace in the West while he crept forward in the East.

Watching the expenditure of the Reichsmark, Hitler held down any increase in wages to the workers. Now he demanded more sacrifices while promising to make Germany economically self-sufficient. One of his propaganda generals declared: "The Soviet Union's government is controlled by Jewish interests and it is money stolen from the Russian people by the Jews which is being used in an attempt to awaken the underworld in all nations to march against European culture and against the holy traditions of all peoples." So long as the French and English rulers believed that Hitler's Reich was saving civilization from the Communists and arming only to protect itself and attack the Soviet Union, Hitler and his Italian ally, Mussolini, could go from victory to victory.

The weaknesses of France and Britain became obvious since their governments, even with enormous resources available to them, had no desire to fight. They seemingly preferred to take no stand alongside their allies as long as they believed that they would remain safe in this manner and continue to support the Germans in their plight against Russia. Hitler kept his eyes set as he prepared for an eventual war against the West.

To accomplish results, Hitler knew he needed control of Austria, Czechoslovakia and Poland as protection for Germany's borders. He realized that he also needed the support of the Allies. Hitler met with Mussolini as Mussolini had taken over Austria during his attempt at annexing the North African states. However, Mussolini would not accede to Hitler's request.

An uprising in Austria by a few Austrian Nazis was quickly quelled by Mussolini. Hitler backed off, looking for another way to get what he wanted. Eventually, he agreed to make Italy an ally to

Germany, even though he fully realized that desertion of allies was an old Italian custom. With Italy as an ally, Hitler had gone through the back door to accomplishing a means for securing Austria. He was now ready to expand Germany's territory.

Meeting with Hungarian officials who were pro-Nazi, Hitler convinced them that Germany was about to enter Czechoslovakia. Hungary did not have a problem with this as long as the Reich would protect them against Romania and Yugoslavia. Once Czechoslovakia had been neutralized, the German army could proceed into Austria.

Hitler crossed the bridge at Braunau where, as a youngster, he had often looked over at Germany. He made only one stop while he was there and that was to the graves of his parents. He entered Vienna in triumph on March 14. As a result of this invasion and with knowledge of what Hitler's propaganda machine had promoted, scores of liberals, Socialists and Jews committed suicide. Thousands fled the country. Many more stayed behind and faced persecution, imprisonment or death. Austria was conquered.

The next victim was Czechoslovakia. Hitler would enter the northwestern section of that country known as Sudetenland where there were German speaking citizens of the Czech Republic. The Sudetens had lived there for centuries but had never shown any national allegiance to any North German state.

As Hitler gained an easy entry into Czechoslovakia, Britain refrained from any commitment to defend that country, intimating that Hitler could have what he sought as long as there was no force involved. Again, England acquiesced to German authority.

On June 3 of that year, the English press looked at the take-over as a welcome example of a peaceful change. "It would be a drastic remedy for the present unrest, but something drastic may be needed."

Hitler was determined to destroy Czechoslovakia. If Prague could be persuaded to give up the Sudetenland, which included all the Czech border fortifications, the rest of the country would be indefensible.

Czechoslovakia had a defense agreement with France and with the Soviet Union, which were allied with Romania and Yugoslavia and also connected by that alliance with France to Britain and Poland. Although Hitler would not have been prepared to enter war with any of that combination, he realized that only the Soviet Union was really prepared to come to the defense of Prague. As has been seen in history, France was looking for any way it could to avoid its obligations in circumstances such as these.

Hitler needed to get the West on his side. His resolution was to create a panic of impending war initiated by the Czech Republic. Each day, Nazi newspapers and radio stations flooded the public with outrageous stories claiming Czech wrath against its people, or about barbaric persecutions, or the menace to society of the Communist regime.

In response, Britain's Lord Chamberlain met with Hitler in Munich. Here he discovered that Hitler was contemplating an immediate invasion. Chamberlain knew that this meant force would be involved unless Czechoslovakia relented and gave in to German demands to release itself to the Reich. Chamberlain returned to London and expressed the demands made by Hitler and his threat of immediate war. When word got out, the Czech army was mobilized. France ordered a partial mobilization as well. Gas masks were distributed in London. Air raid shelters were quickly built in London's public parks.

Hitler continued with his threats as he stated, "If this problem is solved, there will be no further territorial problems in Europe for Germany. We do not want any Czechs. We are resolved!" As Hitler stated in 1936 as an affirmation to his beliefs in the way he led his Third Reich, "Go the way that Providence dictates with the assurance of a sleepwalker."

A meeting was called with Chamberlain, Hitler, Daladier of France, and Mussolini in the Munich *Fuhrerhaus*. Czech representatives were made to wait in an anteroom off the meeting room. Shortly after midnight all four leaders attached their signatures to a document allowing German forces to occupy Czech territory. Prague yielded to what would be a death sentence for their country.

Chamberlain returned home after signing a pledge with Hitler to never go to war again. His ego was inflated as he told the people of Britain that he had saved Czechoslovakia and brought them peace with honor. He fully believed that he had brought peace for their time.

The Peace Accord of Munich was Hitler's greatest triumph of strategy to date. In truth, it was the pinnacle of appeasement and the warrant of death for the Western powers. It was amazing how Hitler's genius lay in his ability to persuade the worthless leaders of the West

49

that they should allow him the means by which he could bring them to devastation. That all these things would eventually take place showed Hitler's cleverness and also showed the incredible stupidity of the Western people who were ready to accede to somebody's demands.

On April 28, 1939, Hitler denounced the British-German Naval Accord and the Polish non-aggression Pact. On May 22, he concluded his treaty of alliance with Italy. Hitler then made a non-aggression pact with the Soviet Union. This connection made with the seat of Communism astounded the Western powers after all the rhetoric stated by Hitler against the evils of that form of government. This move with the East was a means of avoiding the danger of a two-front war, the same as that which brought the Second Reich to disaster.

Stalin did not foresee that Hitler would eventually break this pact and attack the Soviet Union as soon as his purpose had been achieved. Even the powers in the West did not see this coming.

Poland was now the next victim to fall to Germany's Reich. Hitler began a campaign of hatred and fear, fabricated by the Nazi regime, that would be even more devastating than the one he had perpetrated against Czechoslovakia just a year before. The *Genie*, as explained in the Introduction, is in full control.

Once again Chamberlain addressed Hitler over what was now becoming blatantly apparent. He stated that should Germany invade Poland, England would come to Poland's support. But Britain preferred a negotiated settlement.

In his reply to Chamberlain, Hitler insisted that there were necessary land concessions that were needed by Germany. However, he did not want to jeopardize the British-German friendship that he had enjoyed. Further, he stated that if the Reich's demands led to war with Britain, it would be Britain's fault.

Taking advantage of the delay created by the supposed attempts to work out a settlement, Hitler went ahead with the invasion of Poland with all the force he could muster. All Polish fortifications were destroyed as tanks and armored vehicles as well as bombs dropped by the German air command tore through the cities and towns of that country. Air fields, railways and mobilization centers were attacked and annihilated. Even non-combatants were hit with fire, bullets and bombs.

Poland crumpled like a deflated balloon. Within two weeks, all the western provinces were lost, Warsaw was surrounded, and the cabinet was fleeing toward Romania. Artillery and dive-bombers nearly demolished the capitol. In three weeks Poland was owned by Germany.

On September 3, Britain and France declared war on Germany. In less than two weeks time, Russia ordered the Red Army to enter Poland to stop the Germans from taking everything for themselves. Hitler made a concession to Russia and divided the country in two, keeping the western half with all its industrial areas, and giving Russia all the farm lands to the east.

On April 9, 1940, Hitler struck his first great blow at the West. German troops invaded Denmark, a country with whom Hitler had entered a ten-year non-aggression pact just ten months prior. Using this as a jumping-off spot, Hitler's troops crossed into Norway without one shot being fired and without any hindrance as the Norwegians were not prepared for a sneak attack. The Germans had planted agents in the military to assure that there would be no resistance so that no shots would be fired when the German invasion took place. I always found it intriguing that the German agent who directed the military lived less than ten miles from my mother's home. Two kingdoms were conquered in a single day. In his wisdom, Hitler stated in 1925, "The broad mass of a nation will more easily fall victim to a big lie than to a small one."

On May 10, 1940, Germany struck directly at the West. Within hours German forces occupied Luxemburg and raided the Netherlands, Belgium and northern France. Germany had one great advantage. It had infiltrated these areas with spies, traitors, Fifth Columnists and German 'tourists.' Battles were lost seemingly before they had begun. In France, the German armored divisions accompanied by dive-bombers cut the French armies to ribbons. Following the invasion, Hitler toured Paris and visited the tomb of Napoleon. Italy, not wanting to be left out and desiring to be in on the kill, entered the war. The French Republic collapsed.

All that was left now for Germany to conquer was Britain. But, in 1940, Hitler was, like Napoleon, stopped by the Channel. His only means of forcing Britain to succumb was by creating a diversion in which America would be involved in war. This would satisfy

Hitler's greatest obstacle: it would keep the United States from helping Britain if it were under attack half way around the world.

In September of 1940, Hitler arranged a Triple Alliance Pact in which Rome, Berlin and Tokyo agreed to threaten America with war in order to realize their ultimate aspirations for world peace. This was part of what Hitler called his New World Order. However, the United States was not impressed and increased its aid to both Britain and China.

When Hitler realized that nothing was about to change he determined that his best bet was to continue the war in the Mediterranean. Britain, for the moment, could wait.

Italy, in an attempt to look good to its German counterpart, would attack Greece and take control of it as a show to Hitler that it was also a powerful force with which to deal. On October 28, 1940, as Mussolini made demands upon the Greek General, who was also the Greek Prime Minister, as the Italian troops entered Greece from Albania and Italian planes bombed Greek towns, the Italian minister was turned back by the Greeks. Further, the Greek Army then entered Albania and victoriously ran the Italian Army out. At the same time, Britain's Mediterranean fleet, which had been using Greek military bases, pounded into smithereens all the units of the Italian Navy that had been in that area.

On the first day of March, 1941, Bulgaria became the fourth junior member of the Triple Alliance. Two hours later German divisions crossed the Danube and rushed to the Greek and Turkish borders. By March 3rd, when Bulgarians celebrated the anniversary of their liberation from the Turks, the Germans had the country firmly in their grip. As a result, Yugoslavia was now totally encircled.

The Luftwaffe and the Panzer divisions struck at Yugoslavia. Belgrade was in German hands a week after this latest blitz began. The Yugoslav Army, poor in all the weapons of modern warfare and permeated with traitors, crumbled at every point. Many of its rulers as well as its citizens fled to Greece.

Of course, against Hitler's machines, the Greeks were helpless, even with the assistance that the British sent from Egypt. The main body of the invaders poured into Athens within three days of the entrance of Germany into Greece.

The incursion of Yugoslavia and Greece cost the invaders only 2559 killed, 5820 wounded and 3169 missing. Taken by the German Army as prisoners were 344,000 Serbs, 218,000 Greeks and 11,000 British – most of those came from Australia and New Zealand. The British also suffered other losses: four transport ships and two destroyers and a number of smaller vessels were demolished by air attacks over the Mediterranean.

Hitler had taught the world to expect of him only the unexpected. Yet, the world, to its shame was slow to learn.

To invade Britain at this point would be far more difficult than it would have been a year before. Britain's defenders were now rearmed. The Royal Air Force was far more formidable. The British fleet still commanded the northern seas, despite the triumphs of the U-boats, bombers and surface raiders in sinking half a million tons of merchant shipping a month. Instead, Germany would focus its attention on one of their allies: Russia.

On the first Sunday of summer, 1941, the bombers of the Luftwaffe roared out of their hidden hangers along the eastern reaches of the Reich to rain death on the Soviet frontiers. In the Soviet borderlands, as on a dozen other fields, the Luftwaffe and the Panzer divisions cut through the lines of the defenders and raced forward to outflank, encircle and destroy. An immense Soviet army was enveloped and obliged to surrender. The road to Moscow was now clear; the broken Red armies fled everywhere in disorder.

Then, amazingly, all across the hot and dusty Russian plains, vast armies moved out to face the invaders. The two weeks respite gained by earlier annexations made possible full Soviet mobilization. The philosophy of the defending army was the creed of attack. Their weapons were thousands of tanks and planes and heavy guns, wielded with great ability and courage. Their men had faith and a will to fight. When trapped, they resisted like tigers. When free, they slashed at the German divisions with skillfulness and a fury of fanaticism equal to their enemy. When they retreated, they destroyed all in their path and left thousands of guerrilla fighters in the forests and swamps to attack their enemy's rear. The blitz by the Germans had failed. The central armies made no progress toward Moscow. The Red Army was still intact. The strategists who had smashed all the other armies of the Continent in battles of a few weeks duration had finally met their match.

The German Army had inflicted heavy losses on the Red Army and had occupied valuable areas and industrial centers. But its own divisions had suffered tremendously. Its war was no longer a blitz but a contest of exhaustion. Red tanks and guns, though destroyed or captured by thousands, continued to cut down the invaders. The Red air force, seemingly annihilated at the beginning of the struggle, rained death on the German soldiers and even bombed major German cities. Add to this the fact that all over conquered Europe men and women were finding new courage to risk their lives by shooting German officers, blowing up bridges, wrecking trains and summoning their fellows to revolt against Hitler and his followers. Could the Reich for which Hitler had promised a life of a thousand years suffer a demise? It could and would unless the freemen of the West once more shirked their duty. Here was Hitler's last hope. Democratic irresponsibility and blindness had raised the Nazi realm to the heights from which its leaders saw all the world below them ripe for looting. Democratic irresponsibility and blindness might yet deliver all of that world into the hands of the hosts of darkness.

It is interesting to note that while the war was raging in Germany, Hitler made preparations for whatever the outcome might be by hiding enormous sums of wealth in obscure locations. His thoughts were that once he had won the war and the Third Reich was ready for implementation, he would have all the capital needed to build his empire. Proof of this was uncovered following the outcome of the war.

Nazi Germany, during the war years, confiscated approximately $580 million in gold, now worth about 5.6 billion dollars, from some six million people. The gold bullion, gold coins, as well as currency from central banks, silver, diamonds and jewelry was taken from the Jews, many of whom were Hungarian, who were interred in the extermination and concentration camps in 1944. This loot was placed onto rail cars known as the 'Gold Train' and was destined for the Nazi stronghold in the Swiss Alps. With many delays and confusion, as well as being hidden in a tunnel for months, these treasures were eventually en route to Austria when the war ended. After the corrupt Hungarian and German leaders, the Nazis, American and French armies, a few Jewish leaders, the French Security Agency and some international refugee organizations dipped their hands into the treasure-trove, the value diminished to between five and six million dollars in value. To this day, the amount is in dispute as far as content and restitution. The neutral or non-belligerent countries accepted over 300 million dollars in gold bullion, with a current value at this time of 2.6 billion dollars, in exchange for vital goods and raw material from such countries as Spain, Switzerland, Portugal, Italy, Sweden, Norway and Argentina. Switzerland was most prominent in procuring the gold plunder of $580 million and placing it in the Swiss Nation's bank account. The rest went into the accounts of other countries.

After the war, less than 20 million dollars in looted gold was returned by the neutrals. Switzerland only gave back 58 million dollars of the stolen booty. To some, these were the spoils of war, but most of this treasure was the personal property of the victims. It is interesting to note that during the war, Portugal and Spain provided nearly all of the tungsten to produce weapons grade steel. Sweden produced iron ore and lethal gas as well as ball bearings. Turkey produced 100% of chromite to harden steel for armor. All of these items were paid for by the stolen gold from wedding bands, rings, and gold teeth.

The man who acquired the Jewish assets for the German SS under Himmler was Kurt Becker, a colonel in the SS. It was alleged that Becker hid most of the loot and when he died in 1995 in Germany, he was found to be extremely wealthy. His associate, a man named Kasztner, was shot to death by a Holocaust surviver in 1957. We truly live in a mad, mad world where greed takes over.

In March, 1945, American troops, passing through the town of Merkens discovered a salt mine 1200-feet underground. In it they found 100 tons of gold bullion, twenty-nine rows of sacks of gold coins, and balls of international currency, including two-million US dollars. They also found 1000 rare paintings including those of Raphael and Rembrandt. They also came across the suitcases that had belonged to people who had been deported to concentration camps. The total value of these treasures in 1945 amounted to more than three billion dollars. The salt mines made for a great protection to the items in this depository.

Another interesting fact is that the US uses a salt mine in Carlsbad, New Mexico for the storage of plutonium – contaminated nuclear waste that will remain toxic for the next 240,000 years. A similar project was initiated in 1979 in southern Louisiana and east Texas for the storage of oil. However, when it was noticed that the drums could not be sealed in the way that these other treasures and the nuclear waste was sealed, the project was scrapped and any further idea abandoned.

On April 12,1945,President Franklin D. Roosevelt died in Warm Springs, Georgia and Vice-president Harry S. Truman was sworn in as President. Less than three weeks later, on May 7, 1945 at 2:40 a.m., Hitler committed suicide and Germany signed the surrender. The central question by Roosevelt after his February, 1945 Yalta meeting on the Black Sea between Stalin and Churchill was: Would Germans return to another Hitler or be directed to democracy? That same question confronted Harry Truman at his meeting with Churchill and Stalin at Potsdam during their seventeen-day conference that ran through part of July and August.

On July 21,1945, Truman was told by his aide that the US military had successfully completed their testing of the atomic bomb. Truman told his aide that the news gave him a new feeling of confidence. He knew that with the US as sole possessor of this bomb, it would end the Japanese war fast without Russian or British help, and give America power over the postwar world.

Truman was now the most powerful man on earth. He wanted Russia and Britain to approve a plan that would punish Germany and quell any desire to start another war, and yet, still feed and warm Europe.

On the evening of July 31, 1945, Truman gave the formal approval to drop the first atomic bomb on Japan. Truman later told Stalin but he already knew. His order had been to proceed with the bombing after he left Potsdam but no sooner than August 2, 1945.

As stated earlier, on August 6, 1945, the first atomic bomb was dropped on Japan followed by the second bomb on August 9. In response, Japan signed an unconditional surrender.

The signing of the Potsdam Agreement between Russia, Britain and the United States declared that during the occupation, Germany would be treated as a single economic unit with each occupying power to take reparation from its own zone.

Truman's speech to the citizens of the United States outlined what the Potsdam declaration was intended to accomplish. It was designed to eliminate Nazism, armaments, and the war industry. It was then to rebuild democracy by controlling German education, reorganizing local government, and reestablishing a judiciary. It was to grant free press, free speech, freedom of religion and the rights of labor. However, Truman's speech was largely obscured as the unresolved questions and hard compromises that were the legacy of Potsdam were never answered. The end result for all three parties involved in the Potsdam conference was that each side paid what it had to pay to get what it wanted most. Russia got approximately 25% of pre-World War II German territory for Poland. Britain and America were spared the staggering reparations and debt of postwar Germany.

Most of the stolen gold was discreetly sold on the world market. Prior to 1945, it was melted down into gold bars because gold knows no owner. This was to assist in paying for the Nazi war effort.

In 1950, the US Federal Reserve conceded that they did not ask any questions about the origin of gold that was moved from Swiss hands to other nations and which ended up in the Federal Reserve vaults. A request was made by CitiBank of New York to the Treasury Department to have the gold re-melted and then stamped by the Federal Reserve and reissued so that it could be used as collateral to finance the purchase of the ITT International Telephone System from Spain, which was received in the late 1940's from Germany. Some of the gold from Spain was later melted and reissued as 1937 Prussian Mint bars.

Switzerland's role in World War II ended as it became one of the wealthiest nations in Europe. They had played both sides during the war. They were supposed to be a friend of the Allies but they supplied Germany with two billion kilowatt hours of electricity each year during the war. They also allowed their rail system to transport German troops as well as Holocaust victims. They helped protect the enemy's investments, supplied boats for the transport of goods as well as allowed their rail system to transport coal and goods. They also provided arms, ammunition, aluminum, machines, precision tools and agricultural products. It seemed that being neutral really paid off.

In the mid-1980's, I changed hats once again. I had been working for Prudential Insurance but following an interesting offer I went to work for Doctor Sandor Mihaly, the chairman of the world's largest private Swiss Trust. His father had operated this trust in the 1920's, 30's and early 40's. When he died during a botched surgical operation, his son, Sandor, took over the trust. He told me about the history of the trust. They would take deposits of large sums of money and gold from English royalty and society along with that of Saudi royalty from the United Arab Emirates and other Arab states, as well as from Hungary and the German Nazis. The entrusted gold was deposited in vaults located at the airport in Zurich. In later years they did the same for Japan. All were held in typical numbered accounts so as to not be traceable. They never invested funds but only had the use of the cash for purchasing currency and bonds. The chairman, Sandor, was a medical scientist who wanted to use these funds to build hospitals, clinics, and non-military projects. He never could release the funds. My job was to do the research to justify these investments. All it was was a game to keep himself busy.

The attitude of the Swiss is to use caution in everything. Look at projects from all angles and be sure to be familiar with the downside of every task in event of any unknowns as well as the upside as far as any benefits. Always look twice and never rush into any deal. Mihaly went to extremes in his wariness. In any coalition, he would not foster any trust until he had his private investigators check everyone out. That included me when I first started to do work for him. He demanded a detailed report on the person being investigated, including his family and friends. He had people followed to insure their trustworthiness. I know because I was one who had been followed when I acted as a monetary courier for him and his business took me to Japan, the Bahamas, and the Middle East.

Doctor Sandor Mihaly and his wife, Maria, were officially invited to America by President Ronald Reagan. They paid a visit to him at the White House. Of course, there was a subtle suggestion that he bring the Swiss Trust with him. The Doctor and his wife both became US citizens as they had faith in the American Constitution. I know this to be true because he often quoted parts of it to me over the years of our connection. The one thing he did not trust was American business and the lack of ethics in our country. He always exercised great caution in all of his dealings, especially in the United States. [6]

CHAPTER FOUR – FRANCE

"She found a little bottle, and tied round the neck of the bottle was a paper label, with the words, 'DRINK ME,' beautifully printed on it in large letters. It was all very well to say 'Drink me,' but the wise little Alice was not going to do that in a hurry. 'No, I'll look first,' she said, 'and see whether its marked 'poison' *or not;' for she had read several nice little stories about children who had got burnt, and eaten up by wild beasts, and other unpleasant things, all because they* would *not remember the simple rules their friends had taught them: such as, that a red-hot poker will burn you if you hold it too long; and that, if you cut your finger very deeply with a knife, it usually bleeds; and she had never forgotten that, if you drink much from a bottle marked 'poison,' it is almost certain to disagree with you, sooner or later. However, this little bottle was not marked 'poison,' so Alice ventured to taste it, and, finding it very nice (it had, in fact, a sort of mixed flavor of cherry-tart, custard, pineapple, roast turkey, toffy, and hot buttered toast), she very soon finished it off... 'What a curious feeling!' said Alice. 'I must be shutting up like a telescope!' And so it was indeed: she was now only ten inches high. She felt a little nervous about this; 'for it might end, you know,' said Alice to herself, 'in my going out altogether, like a candle. I wonder what I should be like then?' And she tried to fancy what the flame of a candle looks like after the candle is blown out, for she could not remember ever having seen such a thing."* [1]

The community of nations is a jungle. Its law is the law of force: let those take who have the power, let those keep who can. Neighbors are not friends but foes, quick to take advantage of every weakness. Those who forget these things are lost.

The French nation-state is, with the possible exception of England, the oldest of the Great Powers in the Western State System. In its early history, England, separated by the Channel, was not able to act effectively on the Continent after her knights and barons were driven out. The same conflict which ousted England from the mainland launched France on her career as the largest, richest, and most populous State of Europe. From 1500 to 1815 French kings, statesmen, and patriots took pride in the fact that la belle France was ranked first among the nations in military might, in diplomatic prestige, and in the arts of civilization. However, the Franco-Prussian War in the late 1800's spelled the end of French supremacy on the Continent.

In 1918, after four years and three months of bloodshed, France achieved the goal which her diplomats and soldiers had so long pursued. German military and naval strength was reduced to impotence by the Treaty of Versailles. The French Army became, once again, the most powerful force on the Continent. French power and prestige were restored.

The French Government, between 1918 and 1924, insisted upon the full execution of the economic and financial clauses of the Treaty. A weak Germany could perhaps pay no reparations, but a strong Germany could threaten French security. Further measures were adopted to keep Germany impotent as corresponding measures were devised to keep France powerful. New fortifications were erected along the eastern frontier. The French Army, though reduced in numbers, was maintained at what was believed to be the highest possible level of technical efficiency. During the ensuing years, France became complacent, smug and unworried.

By the middle 1930's the power which Paris had once wielded with so little wisdom was all but completely dissipated.

The Frenchmen of the Right who feared the poor, admired Hitler and Mussolini for fighting Communism and keeping the poor in their place. The Frenchmen of the Left who feared the rich, were sworn to peace and filled with deep suspicion of the wealthy. When either group urged action to protect French interests, the other accused it of interventionism, war-mongering and treason. All were agreed that France must fight if France were invaded. However, all were equally agreed that enforcement of the Treaty of Versailles was not worth a war. Not Locarno, nor Ethiopia, nor Spain, nor Austria, nor Czechoslovakia, nor Danzig. These were other people's wars. Being self-righteous and apathetic would be France's doom.

The year 1933 brought a period of disaster in French diplomacy. The French refused to act against the Third Reich even though there were concerns over the ever-growing Nazi movement and the strides being made against other countries. In an effort to keep the German forces in check, the Maginot Line, a wall of steel and concrete, dotted with subterranean batteries and machinegun nests, was rushed to completion along the German frontier.

There was also an unstable balance between the political extremes in parliament. The rise of Fascism was a further source of confusion along with the impact of the Great Depression on French economy.

The fear of Fascism was accelerated when Fascist riots broke out in Paris and drew the powerful Socialist and Communist parties together into an anti-Fascist coalition.

The Third French Republic entered upon its last war under leaders who were totally inept. Its citizens were confused, baffled, and hopelessly divided against themselves. They were a prime target for the Third Reich. No one was enthusiastic for a war against the foe across the Rhine. Originally, the French had felt a degree of confidence believing that the Maginot Line was impregnable. Their belief was soon to be destroyed. Years later, in 1962, Charles deGaulle made a statement that fit the history of this time. His comment was, "How can you govern a country, which has 246 varieties of cheese?"

The rulers of France, members of the powerful Vichy Party, had made a decision based upon their greater worry over the encroaching German Army. They agreed to deceive London and Washington as long as possible by bringing Allied and American shipments useful to the Reich to French ports. The French would then join Hitler in striking blows against Britain and the United States. Such deception, if successful, would lead Hitler to curb Mussolini's anti-French ambitions and would bring the reward of a favored place for France in a Nazi world. Hitler had other ideas.

France of 1940 died with little bloodshed. Some 150,000 French soldiers were slain or wounded by the Germans and by France's own lack of weapons as well as by the incompetence or treason of their commanders, and by their unwillingness to fight for a cause already betrayed by their leaders. Under the machine-guns and bombs of Nazi flyers some tens of thousands of civilians perished. In the aftermath, the Republic died and France perished as a power and as a free state. DeGaulle was later heard to say in 1940, "Since they whose duty it was to wield the sword of France have let it fall shattered to the ground, I have taken up the broken blade."

It took time for the French to realize that their collaboration with Germany was folly. All of their power and so-called freedoms were taken away one by one. Parties were forbidden to hold meetings. Payment of members of Parliament was suspended. Commissars of public power were named to ferret out secret societies and oppositionists. Special courts were set up for political offenders.

This repression built resentment. Acts of sabotage increased. Rioting broke out in Paris. A German officer was stabbed to death in a subway. Thousands of Jews and Communists were arrested. It was not long before the guillotine and the firing squad were called into action. The Gestapo executed innocent hostages for every new attack on German troops.

In the long darkness of defeat, the men and women of the dead Republic drank shame and tasted despair. They had loved peace not wisely but too well. They had cherished their way of life too little to risk their lives to keep it. They had abandoned Europe to save France. They had therefore lost France and lost peace and their happiness as well.

CHAPTER FIVE – ENGLAND

" 'Flamingoes and mustard,' said the Duchess, 'both bite. And the moral of that is – Birds of a feather flock together.' 'Only mustard isn't a bird,' Alice remarked. 'Right, as usual,' said the Duchess: 'what a clear way you have of putting things!' 'It's a mineral, I think,' said Alice. 'Of course it is,' said the Duchess, who seemed ready to agree to everything that Alice said. 'There's a large mustard-mine near here. And the moral of that is – The more there is of mine, the less there is of yours.' 'Oh, I know!' exclaimed Alice, who had not attended to this last remark. 'It's a vegetable. It doesn't look like one, but it is.' 'I quite agree with you,' said the Duchess; 'and the moral of that is – Be what you would seem to be – or, if you'd like it put more simply – Never imagine yourself not to be otherwise than what it might appear to others that what you were or might have been was not otherwise than what you had been would have appeared to them to be otherwise.' "[1]

England, like France, caused its own misery. It was self-inflicted. It came from a long history of blunders all created by the people who ruled the kingdom. Even though peace and prosperity was the focus of their attention, they managed to lose both. How? By minding their own business and keeping out of other people's wars. In 1931, the error of England's ways came to light when the country's confused voters granted their trust to the ultra-Tory wing of the Conservative Party. It gained domination without any challenge. This was a regime of blind men was the precursor to a leadership that brought England to the brink of disaster in May of 1940; a disaster that was the fruit of its folly.

The greatest error of Tory politics was the ignoring of a principle, which the wise leaders of the past centuries used to protect England and to keep it powerful. That principle was to maintain pressure within all the European countries in order to retain a balance of power on the Continent. Such a balance was the result of giving diplomatic and military support to its neighbors. Britain had waged war in the past during the years between 1815 and 1904 only when and where it was needed so that it could maintain its isolationism. When the growing power of the Second Reich threatened the Continent, Britain joined forces with France and Russia to try and control Berlin. Yet even when joined by Japan and Italy they were inadequate to defeat Germany. The only way that victory was able to come to the Continent in 1918 was when the United States came to their aid. During the ensuing years, Britain's leaders forgot that victory and went so far as to allow the Third Reich to increase its power to a point where it could conquer the Continent and make threats against Britain.

The question of why Britain's leaders so completely forgot the lessons of the past carries various answers. Firstly is the fact that Downing Street supported the League of Nations half-heartedly and allowed itself to follow a line of appeasement. This relaxation of the rules was the primary fault that led to the weakening of England's government. Secondly, Britain supported Germany and the Third Reich against France. This alienated the Soviet Union. Thirdly, it firmly declined all obligations to defend Vienna, Prague and Warsaw.

This mad, or muddled, suicide policy was due to a logic that presupposed a power alliance between Japan and the USSR in Asia and a similar alliance between the Third Reich and the USSR in Europe in which they were likely to checkmate each other. Therefore, Britain could stand aside and watch so as to protect itself from involvement: the wisdom of appeasement. The only difficulty was that this logic was tragically false.

The Tory politicians looked without seeing and listened without hearing. As an example, Member of Parliament, Sir Thomas Moore, said, "If I may judge from my personal knowledge of Herr Hitler, peace and justice are the key words of his policy." This was followed by another Member of Parliament, Sir Arnold Wilson, who stated, "There is no militarism in Germany. There is almost no great power with which we are less likely to become involved in war with than Germany." Plutocrats, lords and clerics flocked with enthusiasm into such organizations as the Anglo-German Fellowship, The Link, the Friends of Italy and the Friends of National Spain. Sir Thomas Inskip, Minister for Coordination of Defense, held that Britain should not insist upon the withdrawal of Italian troops from Spain, "before they have finished the work they were sent there to do." Lord Mount Temple, at a dinner of the Anglo-German Fellowship: "Unity is essential and the real danger to the world today does not come from Germany or Italy but from Russia." Lord Londonderry, Minister for Air, was "at a loss to understand why we could not make common ground in some form or other with Germany in opposition to

Communism. The anti-Communist platform was and still is invaluable."

British policy became a prime case in point of the blind leading the blind. The questionable course of British diplomacy in the 1930's, from Sir John Simon's rape of Manchuria to Sir Neville Chamberlain's betrayal of Ethiopia, Spain, Austria and Czechoslovakia was a product of the Tory mind. During the early part of this period of time several changes took place in the British Parliament. Interest swayed from liberalism to conservatism and back again as the financial conditions in England changed. Before long a new Prime Minister, Stanley Baldwin, was elected; a man more interested in the moral state of affairs in Britain than in the political nature of its position in the world. His greatest triumph was the abdication of King Edward VIII, who succeeded his father, George V, in January of 1936 and left his throne to his brother, George VI, in December when Baldwin forbade him to marry the American divorcee, Mrs. Wallis Simpson. Baldwin's next greatest triumph was his successful befuddlement of the British public regarding all issues of war and peace all through the course of his diplomatic muddling in dealing with Hitler and Mussolini. Baldwin stated on the eve of Hitler's repudiation of the military clauses of Versailles that Hitler would soon be in full possession of his normal strength; he completed his thought with, "One of the greatest perils that have met democracies in the past, and meets them today, is when their leaders have not the courage to tell them the truth." A year later, following his election, he confessed, "Suppose I had gone to the country and said that Germany was rearming and that we must rearm. Does anybody suppose that this pacific country would have rallied to that at that moment? I cannot think of anything that would have made the loss of the election from my point of view more certain."

At the end of May, 1937, Baldwin was succeeded by Neville Chamberlain as Prime Minister. Like his father, Joseph Chamberlain, he served as Mayor of Birmingham before entering national politics. He essentially was a cold businessman who made screws, nuts and guns. His passion was peace. His political technique, like that of Baldwin, was spreading confusion. Accordingly, the betrayal of China was for business. The desertion of Ethiopia and the League of Nations was for peace. Connivance in the murder of the Spanish Republic was non-intervention. Cooperation in Fascist aggression was appeasement.

What Ralph Waldo Emerson said of their predecessors could easily apply to Britain's sorry leaders of the 1930's: "Truth in private life, untruth in public, marks these home-loving man. Their political conduct is not decided by general views, but by internal intrigues and personal and family interests. They cannot readily see beyond England, nor in England can they transcend the interests of the governing classes. Their mind is in a state of arrested development."

Appeasement had been suggested and the British public accepted this policy in the mistaken conviction that it provided the only escape from war. The public did not, at the outset, accept this course and, in fact, was tricked into supporting those who did. Between 1934 and 1935, a poll was conducted under Lord Robert Cecil. It was a National Peace Ballot in which no less than 11,500,000 votes were cast with an overwhelming majority supporting the League of Nations and the disarmament of aggressors and including economic and military sanctions. Baldwin declared, "We value this support." This was followed by an election poster with Baldwin's fist squarely printed on the Peace Covenant with the caption, "Our word is our bond." In the election of November 15, 1935, the government won 431 out of 615 seats in the House of Commons. This was a popular endorsement not of appeasement but of collective security to which the government had pledged itself. The voters did not know that Baldwin aids made a secret pact at Geneva in September to betray Ethiopia and the League of Nations. This leaked out three weeks after the election. For the next four years a group of leaders, placed in power by a public convinced it was supporting the cause of world order and resistance to Fascist aggression, pursued a policy of connivance in aggression, which was certain to produce world anarchy. These leaders progressively sold this policy to the public in the name of peace.

Only one voice was raised in protest and warning to all that was taking place in England. Each time it was ignored by those who knew better. It was the voice of a very rare character, a Tory dissenter by the name of Winston Churchill. At each step in world decisions, the appeasers told Parliament and the public that their actions would insure peace.

The formula for Britain was to be no commitments and no entanglements. A clear indication was given to Berlin, according to

Sir Anthony Eden, Prime Minister, that Downing Street would not resist German expansion to the East.

Anthony Eden further stated that British arms would never be used in a war of aggression. If the occasion arose they would be used in Britain's defense and in the defense of the territories of the British Commonwealth of Nations. If the occasion arose they would be used in defense of France and Belgium against unprovoked aggression in accordance with England's existing treaty obligations. If a new Western European settlement were to be reached, they would be used in the defense of Germany were she the victim of unprovoked aggression by any of the other signatories of such a settlement. These, together with the Treaty of Alliance with Iraq and with Egypt, would be their definite obligations.

Britain should assume no commitments to defend victims of aggression in eastern or central Europe. This was the only assurance, which the leaders of the Third Reich required; this gave Hitler a free hand in the East. Britain insisted that Nazi imperialism must achieve its purposes without war, since war might involve Britain by involving France. In 1938, Neville Chamberlain said, "How horrible, fantastic, incredible it is that we should be digging trenches and trying on gas masks here because of a quarrel in a far away country between people of whom we know nothing." In September of that same year, he also said, "This is the second time in our history that there has come back from Germany to Downing Street peace with honour. I believe it is peace for our time."

These implementations were met with only one voice raised against them and that was by Alfred Duff-Cooper, First Lord of the Admiralty. He said in the House of Commons, "It was not for Serbia or Belgium we fought in 1914, though it suited some people to say so, but we were fighting then, as we should have been fighting recently, in order that one great power should not be allowed, in disregard of treaty obligations and the laws of nations and against all morality, to dominate by brutal force the continent of Europe."

This was followed by a statement by Winston Churchill: "We have sustained a total, unmitigated defeat. We are in the presence of a disaster of the first magnitude which has befallen Great Britain and France. Do not let us blind ourselves. Do not suppose that this is the end. It is only the beginning. It is only the foretaste of the bitter cup which will be proffered to you year after year unless by a supreme recovery of moral health and marital vigor we rise again to take our stand for freedom, as in olden times." Unfortunately, no one cared.

On March 31, 1939, the British Government agreed to give Poland all the support in its power in the event of any action which clearly threatened Polish independence, and which the Polish Government accordingly considered it vital to resist with their national forces. Poland would, likewise, consider itself under an obligation to render assistance to Great Britain under the same conditions.

For the first time in twenty years, Britain had entered into a bilateral pledge of mutual defense with an Eastern European State.

On April 13, 1939, the Government of Britain was prepared to lend Greece and Romania all the support in its power in the event any action being taken which clearly threatened the independence of either, and which the Greek or Romanian Governments respectively considered it vital to resist with their national forces.

On October 19, 1939, Turkey signed a fifteen-year treaty of mutual assistance with Britain and France who pledged aid to Ankara in case of attack by any European power. All agreed to aid one another in case of aggression by a European power leading to war in the Mediterranean.

This intended coalition failed completely of its purpose. It neither deterred the Axis from risking war nor did it afford to the Western powers any allies sufficiently powerful to save them from defeat. Poland was to be crushed like an eggshell. Romania and Greece had assumed no reciprocal obligations to come to the aid of France and Britain. When Italy invaded Greece, Britain was able, thanks to naval control of the Mediterranean, to come to the aid of Athens and strike heavy blows at the enemy from Greek bases. Even the attack upon Greece did not move Turkey to enter the war. All the Balkan states were lost as a result.

British spokesmen reiterated their willingness to settle all differences through negotiation. They could not see the inevitable, that negotiation was not working. Poland, Romania and Turkey could be protected against the Reich only by the USSR. That the British negotiations with the only power which could have served as an adequate counterweight to the Axis should have come to nothing was not unusual, based upon Britain's leadership. It refused to listen to the repeated warnings during the last spring of peace that all the Cabinet's efforts would be in vain unless the Soviet Union were enlisted in the coalition. But anti-Soviet prejudices were such that a viable bargain with the Kremlin was not possible.

In the tedious discussions that followed, Moscow demanded a binding alliance for mutual defense against any attack or indirect aggression against the Baltic States. Moscow also demanded military access to Polish territory if the USSR was to assume obligations to defend Poland. The House of Commons refused after having sacrificed China, Ethiopia, Spain, Austria, Czechoslovakia, and Albania to the Fascist aggressors. London would make no pact with Moscow. And, since Poland's leaders would rather see their state perish at the hands of Hitler than accept military aid from the hands of Stalin, London could not or would not meet the terms of the USSR.

Rejecting the Kremlin's terms, Stalin made the obvious choice. His non-aggression pact with Berlin of August 23 left the Western powers isolated in the face of a formidable foe.

Never did modern Britain embark upon a war under such perilous circumstances as prevailed in 1939. The cause had already been all but lost at Madrid and Munich and Moscow. To fight the Reich with no allies except for a weak Poland and a defeated France was to invite disaster. Yet not to fight was to invite destruction.

On September 3, a note was delivered to German Charge Kordt, informing him that the two powers were at war on that date and at that time. Poland perished at once.

It was clear that the British Prime Minister, Neville Chamberlain, was losing the war as he had lost the peace. If England still lived, the credit for survival was due to Winston Churchill and to the millions of men and women whom he rallied to devotion and sacrifice in a cause they had all but forgotten under his frail predecessors. The coming to power of this descendant of the Duke of Marlborough symbolized the end of the rule of businessmen and the ascendancy, in the face of disaster, of an elite group of fighters and intellectuals.

Churchill was in his youth a war correspondent in Cuba, in India, in the Sudan, and in South Africa where he was captured by the Boers and escaped from jail. He was familiar with military conflict and was a student of war strategy. As such, he warned his countrymen, always in vain, of their need to arm and to fight before the Nazi Reich should overwhelm them. Of course, they did not listen. In 1937, he stated, "Dictators ride to and fro upon tigers which they dare not dismount. And the tigers are getting hungry."

As England approached the time for battle, Churchill said the battle of France is over. The battle of Britain is about to begin. He continued, "If we can stand up to Hitler all Europe may be freed and the life of the world may move forward into broad sunlit uplands; but if we fail, the whole world, including the United States and all that we have known and cared for, will sink into the abyss of a new Dark Age made more sinister and perhaps more prolonged by the lights of a perverted science.

"Let us therefore brace ourselves to our duty and so bear ourselves that if the British Commonwealth and Empire last for a thousand years, men will still say, 'This was their finest hour.'"

After a summer lull in which military operations paused and obscure peace overtures came to nothing, the German Luftwaffe opened an all out assault on London in the hope of softening England for invasion. Hundreds of bombers made day and night hideous, slaying thousands and tens of thousands of civilians, burning entire blocks of houses, smashing factories, schools, churches, palaces, tenements, and many of the architectural treasures of the centuries. But the people of Britain refused to be terrorized into submission. Their resistance hardened to steel, for they followed a great leader who promised them no comforts and told them no lies.

The Royal Air Force won the battle of London and made invasion too hazardous to attempt. Never before, said Churchill, had so much been owed by so many to so few. By mid-summer 1941, some 50,000 of them had lost their lives in air raids.

Two-thirds of England's millions lived week by week only by foodstuffs brought from abroad in the holds of a thousand ships.

In the battle of the sea, the Royal Navy was able to cut off the Axis powers from most of their sea trade. In the few spectacular sea fights which now and then took place, it tore apart the enemy as it had done in days of old. In mid-December of 1939 three British cruisers drove the formidable pocket-battleship, *Admiral Graf Spee*, into the harbor of Montevideo where her captain scuttled his vessel and took his life rather than renew the engagement. In November of 1940, Sir

Andrew Cunningham's Mediterranean squadron smashed Italy's battleships. In May of 1941, the raiding *Bismarck*, after having destroyed the *Hood*, was similarly trapped and sunk. But in the narrow waters off Norway and Greece the great gray ships of war were checkmated by the Luftwaffe. And in the restless wastes of the North Atlantic Britain's Navy faced a task almost beyond its powers.

Between September and May, 1939-1940, three ships were being sunk for every new one being built in British and American shipyards combined. Losses were reduced by the increased output of destroyers, corvettes, and long-range bombers. As the war's third year began, American patrols off Greenland and Iceland were at last given orders to shoot in their mission of keeping open the sea-lanes. The construction of ships and of yet more ships in all the yards of the Empire and of the New World offered promise of ultimately overtaking the enemy's work of destruction.

Churchill and his people refused to admit defeat.

The battle of East Africa began in August of 1940. Britain entered with a vengeance. By May 1941, on the fifth anniversary of Mussolini's victory over Ethopia, Haile Selassie re-entered his capitol and two weeks later the re-capture of East Africa was over.

British arms fared less well in the struggle for the Islamic countries around the rim of the Eastern Mediterranean. These Arab lands of palm and desert were all once part of the great Mohammedan realm of the Sultans which had stretched from the gates of Vienna to the frontiers of India and from Gibraltar, the Sahara and the Sudan to the Caucasus and the Crimea. Their empire had long since passed into the hands of the British, the French and the Italians. At the outbreak of World War II only three of the Arab States were free of alien rule: Saudi Arabia, Oman and Yemen. Two more enjoyed nominal independence under British treaties of protection: Egypt and Iraq. Here Britain and the Reich waged war for control of the Near East.

The strategic starting place of the East was Turkey. This once proud realm, originally master of all the Arab world, had lost the last of its non-Turkish provinces by sharing in the defeat of the Kaiser's Reich.

Nazi control of the Straits and Anatolia would enable the Reich to dominate the Levant and to descend on Egypt by way of Iraq, Syria and Palestine. British control of Turkey would insure protection of Egypt and the Bible lands and perhaps help to save the Balkans from Nazi domination.

The war for the Moslem world became a series of campaigns around the rim of a circle with Ankara at its center. With the coming of spring in 1941, Nazi forces gathered in Hungary, Romania and Bulgaria to strike toward the Aegean. Other Nazi forces moved across the Mediterranean to reinforce the Italians in Libya. Erwin Rommel ordered his North African Panzer divisions to attack. This allowed Axis troops to reach the border of neutral Egypt. This blow was timed to coincide with the Nazi conquest of Yugoslavia and Greece, and with an Axis overthrow of Iraq. On April 4, Regent Emir Illah and Premier Taha Al-Haschimi were ousted from power in Baghdad by the followers of Rashid Ali Beg Gailani who proposed to liberate his land from British influence by delivering it to the Axis. Haj Amin el

Husseini, exiled Mufti of Jerusalem, issued a summons from Beirut for a Holy War by all of Islam. Berlin and Rome sent military missions to Iraq while the Luftwaffe crossed Syria, occupied the Mosul district and moved toward Baghdad.

Prompt British action by British bombers assured that by the end of May, Baghdad was theirs. The Axis allies fled to Iran along with the Mufti and the Axis diplomats.

In the course of these operations, Syria had given full support to the Axis. The Royal Air Force accordingly bombed Syrian airports where Axis planes had fueled. Syria was invaded from Palestine with other British forces striking westward from Iraq. Hitler was obliged to abandon Syria to its fate in order to launch his invasion of Russia.

The result was an Anglo-Free French victory. Damascus was taken on the day when the forces of the Reich crossed the Soviet frontiers.

When spring turned to summer in 1941 the British Commonwealth of Nations was fighting alone against the most formidable military power of all time. No British territories anywhere in the world, except for the Channel Islands, were held by the enemy. Britain had no allies anywhere in the world, while Hitler had two other great powers. Such was the penalty of the weakness of Britain and their folly diplomacy.

On the eleventh of May the Luftwaffe destroyed the House of Commons, damaged Big Ben, and wrecked Westminster Abbey and Westminster Hall. On the thirty-first of May the Luftwaffe bombed

Dublin, capitol of neutral Eire. It had now reached a point where the British needed American aid if the war was to be won.

On the first summer Sunday of the year, Hitler gave Britain a mighty ally. On the very first day on which Hitler's army was ordered to march against Moscow, Churchill broadcast to the world that Britain would give whatever help it could to Russia and the Russian people. If Hitler thought that his attack on Soviet Russia would cause a division he was mistaken. The Russian danger was Britain's danger and the danger as well to the United States.

On July twelfth an Anglo-Soviet agreement was signed in Moscow. The two governments would give each other assistance and support to destroy Hitler. What British arms could not do, the Red Army did – at least temporarily. Hitler's army was stopped short of a speedy victory.

Russia's resistance and American aid promised to protect the British Isles from starvation or successful invasion. Much more than this was called for. Britain lacked nothing in dogged courage and full willingness to endure all and dare all to the end. But it still lacked vision. And where leaders lack vision, the people perish.

On August ninth to eleventh, Churchill and President Roosevelt met in secrecy in a northern harbor in the Atlantic. Each brought their chiefs of staff. A *communique* issued in London and Washington on August 14, 1941, confirmed the conference in which a declaration was made that both countries would engage in resisting aggression. That was further explained in an eight-point outline of their ultimate purpose. By the majority of Americans and Britons it was a flop. In summary, if people were looking for leadership, this was an empty conference. In effect, those who asked for bread were given a stone. The Britons were waiting for America to realize their duty and come to their aid. Many promises were hinted at but nothing was cast in concrete. This was typical of politicians. Nothing has changed over the years and, obviously, nothing has been learned.

Two months after the outbreak of the Nazi-Soviet war and six weeks after the Anglo-Soviet alliance, London and Moscow took their first joint military step. Early in August 1941, Soviet troops from the north and British troops from the south crossed the Iranian frontiers and took control of the southern oil fields. Both governments issued statements explaining the necessity of military action and pledging respect for Iranian independence and integrity. The Iranian Army offered only token resistance. Anglo-Soviet forces occupied Teheran and cleansed the land of Axis agents. This quick victory improved the Allied position with respect to Turkey and furnished a safe and open southern road for the shipment of troops and supplies to Russia.

On December seventh, 1941, Japan attacked Pearl Harbor and the United States finally entered the war both in Europe and in Asia. The Second World War lasted 2,174 days after starting on September 1, 1939 and ending on August fourteenth, 1945. Britain and America lost one million lives not including those citizens lost during the raids on Britain. Approximately forty-six million lives were lost in the European segment of the war.

Nothing makes sense...other than we live in a mad, mad world.

Martin Olson

CHAPTER SIX – USSR

"'If everybody minded their own business,' the Duchess said, in a hoarse growl, 'the world would go round a deal faster than it does.' 'Which would not be an advantage,' said Alice. 'Just think what work it would make with the day and night! You see the earth takes twenty-four hours to turn round on its axis—' 'Talking of Axes,' said the Duchess, 'chop off her head!' Alice glanced rather anxiously at the cook, to see if she meant to take the hint; but the cook was busily stirring the soup, and seemed not to be listening, so she went on again: 'Twenty-four hours, I think; or is it twelve? I –' 'Oh, don't bother me!' said the Duchess. 'I never could abide figures!'"[1]

Moscow's greatest desire was for peace. The problem was that to them peace meant appeasement rather than conflict.

Appeasement, as practiced in politics, means to seek peace by sacrificing others to aggressors. Appeasement leads to war and brings the appeasers to ruin. During the 1930's the non-Fascist states of the world had to choose between hanging together or hanging separately. Only one great power spoke out against the folly of this course and repeatedly urged united action for joint defense. That power was the Union of Soviet Socialist Republics.

The interests of the USSR in international politics, like those of all other states, reflected the attitudes and values of its ruling class. While capitalist states were dominated politically by nationalistic businessmen or landowners, moved by patriotism and by profit motives, these classes were destroyed in Russia and replaced by a new political elite consisting primarily of middle class intellectuals, but speaking in the name of the poorest of classes.

In March of 1917, Nicholas II, the last of the Romanovs, abdicated his position in favor of a new provisional government composed of middle class democrats and moderate socialists. The Russian Social Democratic party had been split since 1903 into the Menshevik Group and the Bolshevik Group. The Bolshevik Group was led by a man named Vladimir Ilytch Ulianov alias Nikolai Lenin. His collaborator was Len Davidov Bronstein alias Leon Trotsky. These men and their followers went to Russia in the spring of 1917 via the Reich because the German high command was sure that they would complete the disintegration of Russia by winning the support of workers, peasants and soldiers who would support an all-out revolution.

Lenin's Social Democrats began a revolt, which overthrew the existing government, and Lenin was named president. In 1918, the Bolsheviki changed its name to the Communist party in order to distinguish itself from the reformist socialists. The new party was highly organized and intended to prepare the way for a Communistic social order and a classless state.

The Communists viewed their revolution as a step toward world revolution leading to the overthrow of capitalism, nationalism and imperialism. However, with the completion of the armistice on the Eastern front, the peace accord took Russia out of the war. The Soviet government refused to accept the public debts incurred by the former regime. These included pre-war bonds held in enormous amounts by French and British investors and huge war loans extended by Britain, France and the United States. That same government then confiscated foreign property and private investments in Russia. The new regime summoned the workers of the world to revolt and to overthrow capitalistic governments.

In August of 1918, Russia was subject to an allied blockade and military intervention by Czechoslovakians, British, French, American, Japanese and other allied troops. The intervention coincided with counter-revolutionary uprisings within Russia, subsidized and supported by the Allied governments. The Soviet government was assaulted on all sides, within and without. Russia met these threats by forming what it called the Red Terror and by organizing the Red Army. In March, 1919, the Communist party was officially established, with its headquarters in Moscow, as an international federation of the revolutionary Communist parties throughout the world.

The civil strife was long and bloody. In the end the Red Army, directed by Trotsky, proved to be more than a match for its enemies, both domestic and foreign. Peace appeared to be on the horizon.

1921 was the turning point for internal policies and in foreign relations. Six years of battle with neighboring Poland, who wanted to restore its frontiers of 1772, left Russia economically strapped. In the spring of 1921 Britain concluded a trade agreement and the blockade was ended.

In 1922, the European powers demanded payment of Russia's debt, which they claimed was thirteen billion dollars. This was met by a counter-claim from the Soviets stating their demand for sixty billion dollars in damages. Neither side would yield.

Europe, Japan and the United States eyed the Soviet market realizing its potential. As such the Allies eventually cancelled all their former claims. In return for fishing and oil concessions, Japan agreed to recognize Moscow.

With the death of Lenin in 1927, his disciple, Stalin, took control of the party. In 1924, Stalin had said, "The State is an instrument in the hands of the ruling class, used to break the resistance of the adversaries of that class." He was a rival of Trotsky. Stalin led Trotsky to his dismissal and forced him into exile. Stalin then launched a five-year plan in 1928 to provide for a huge industrialization program, which included collectivization of all agriculture. Private trade was outlawed. It was Stalin's position, as he said in 1932, that, "There are various forms of production: artillery, automobiles, lorries. You also produce commodities. There are works and products, such things are highly necessary. Engineering things. For people's souls, products are highly necessary, too. Products are very important for people's souls. You are engineers of human souls." This program grew steadily and paved the way for a second five-year plan.

The triumph of Hitler in Germany in 1933 altered the peace problem of the USSR. The German Communist party, largest in the world outside of Russia, had gone down to defeat after it had fought bitterly with the largest of Socialist parties. Both had been destroyed along with German liberalism. The Nazi leaders were committed to conquest in the East and to an armed crusade against Bolshevism. Militant Fascism threatened Moscow with armed attack and promised to destroy Communists, Socialists and liberals in other states. To prevent any assault from Berlin, Moscow had to arm itself and find allies to back it.

The Franco-Soviet non-aggression pact was supplemented by a commercial treaty. A pact was made with Poland and the Baltic States along with closer relations to Turkey and Great Britain. Czechoslovakia and Romania recognized the USSR, following the example of Hungary. On September 18, 1934, the Soviet Union became a member of the League of Nations. Efforts to conclude a non-aggression pact with Berlin and to induce the Reich to enter into a binding peace agreement failed. So, the USSR became the ally of France and Czechoslovakia, within the framework of the League, to resist Nazi aggression.

In midsummer, 1935, Russia decided to build its internal strength by not continuing any hostilities against the large democratic governments of the people within its borders. Instead, it called upon Socialists and liberals to form a united front opposed to Fascism. Even the Roman Catholics in Germany were invited to join in opposing Nazi rule. Here, Stalin was asked to encourage Catholicism in Russia by way of consoling the pope in 1935. He once stated, "The pope...how many divisions has he got?"

Socialists and liberals greeted this with suspicion as such a move had been made before for the purpose of insuring Communist domination. British Laborites as well as socialists in Czechoslovakia and America declined to cooperate. But in France and Spain, liberals and Socialists joined Communists in popular front movements to resist Fascist attacks on democracy.

Other defensive measures were devised to meet the danger of a possible Japanese attack in the East. Both the USSR and the United States had a common suspicion of Japan. Moscow made repeated but vain efforts to conclude a non-aggression pact with Tokyo. As a conciliatory gesture, the USSR sold the Chinese Eastern Railway to Manchukuo in March, 1935, and in the autumn of 1936 proposed to extend Japanese fishing and oil concessions in eastern Siberia – until the announcement of the German-Japanese anti-Communist accord of November 25 caused a reversal in policy. A self-sufficient Far Eastern army of 250,000 troops was established in the maritime provinces ready to invade Manchukuo should Japan attack. A thousand warplanes were poised to assist in such an attack. Fears of a combined Nazi-Japanese attack, with possible Finnish and Polish support, led to strengthening frontier fortifications in the east and in the west. By January, 1936, the Red Army numbered 1,300,000 men and had some 6,000 tanks and 7,000 warplanes. Every effort was made to increase the output of mechanized armaments.

On December 1, 1934, an aide of Stalin was assassinated in Leningrad. Within a few weeks thereafter, 117 persons were executed as terrorists. As in all dictatorships, ruthless means were held to be justified by ideal ends. But to critics, the ends seem to be destroyed by the means.

Stalin believed in placing internal enemies to the State in prison or in the cemetery. The victims included many who were

91

honest critics of the despot in the Kremlin and many were liquidated out of personal malice. The USSR was not a weak state but a strong one. The result was a slow and secret abandonment of Nazi and Japanese dreams of conquest at the expense of the Soviet State and a reorientation of aggressive designs against the Western powers. Western leaders continued to practice appeasement.

Without the support of the Western powers, Moscow could not thwart Fascist aggression. Without the support of the Western democrats, Communists could not combat Fascist tactics of disintegration in other states. When the USSR sought to use the League to save Ethiopia from Mussolini, London and Paris preferred to save Mussolini at the cost of destroying Ethiopia and the League. When the USSR sought to save the Spanish Republic by observing the non-intervention agreement only in the measure to which it was observed in Rome and Berlin, the Western appeasers preferred to cooperate with the Axis in destroying the Republican regime. The Spanish People's Front died. The French People's Front followed it to the grave. Stalin's one comment at that time was, "There is one eternally true legend, that of Judas."

On March 10, 1939, Stalin spoke to the Communist Party of the USSR. His speech promoted peace with all countries and pledged support of nations resisting aggression. Within a week after Stalin's words were spoken, Hitler liquidated Czechoslovakia and gave Carpatho-Ukraine to Hungary. Both countries, following their respective losses, sought to rebuild a coalition against Germany. The enterprise required Soviet collaboration. But most of the Western leaders were by no means convinced that the Nazi threat was as grave as that stated by Moscow. This attitude confirmed the Kremlin's distrust for the West. British willingness to guarantee Poland, and even Romania and Greece, before coming to terms with the USSR evoked contempt in Moscow.

An alliance with the Western powers could have halted Hitler's career of aggression by threatening him with a two-front war and swift defeat. As a result of mistrust, Moscow blamed London and Paris for the failure, and with much reason. London and Paris, with less reason, believing they knew what was best, blamed Moscow. But assessment of blame was futile. Hitler was the victor. He had once more succeeded in dividing his victims against one another and isolating them, one by one, for the kill.

The Kremlin's policy after the outbreak of hostilities was strict neutrality, tempered by a firm determination to sell non-intervention to Hitler at a price which would greatly strengthen the defenses of the USSR against the Reich. The first step was to seize the former Russian territories of Poland and to reach an agreement with Berlin on its division. On September 28, a new German-Soviet agreement partitioned Poland.

Efforts to negotiate a mutual assistance pact with Turkey failed in the autumn of 1939 because of Ankara's reluctance to meet Soviet terms and Turkish determination to remain faithful to the Western Allies. When Finland rejected similar demands, the Kremlin resorted to force. Moscow saw that without such a pact there was a threat to Leningrad. Russia needed an effective military control of the Gulf of Finland and the entire northwestern frontier.

In November of that year, Russia alleged that Finnish frontier guards had fired on Soviet troops. Finland denied the charge. Moscow retorted by denouncing the Soviet-Finnish non-aggression pact of 1932 and ordered Soviet troops and air forces to attack Finland.

The Finns rallied to the defense of their country and inflicted heavy losses on the inferior Soviet troops sent against them. Over 100,000 lives were lost in bitter fighting in subzero weather.

Finland appealed to the Western powers and to the League of Nations for assistance. What they received was not what they wanted. Finally, the Finnish Government decided that its situation was hopeless. It asked Moscow for terms. And on March 12, 1940, a Finnish delegation in Moscow signed a peace treaty with the USSR. Moscow secured what it was looking for.

The ultimate irony of the Finnish war became apparent only later. Stalin had infuriated the rulers of Finland and then failed to deprive them of their power to take revenge. His reward for moderation was to have Helsinki join Hitler in assaulting the USSR in June of 1941. The moral of this is that in power politics there are no morals.

Neither Hitler nor Stalin was yet prepared to defy the other openly. Each maneuvered for position. Before long a German armored division had landed in Finland. The Kremlin, fearing the worst and hoping for the best, sought safety in new means of appeasement.

On Sunday, June 22, 1941, German troops attacked Russia in a surprise assault. No demands were presented, no ultimatum was delivered, no complaints were made. Hitler had given Moscow no chance to accept or refuse demands. His object was the destruction of the Soviet power.

The desperate struggle across the vast Russian plains in the summer of 1941 was the bitterest and bloodiest combat fought up to this point in World War II. On both sides were enormous casualties.

Early in October of 1941, the Nazi Chancellor claimed 2,500,000 Russian prisoners, 22,000 guns, 18,000 tanks, 14,500 planes were captured or wrecked. However, he admitted, Germany had no idea how gigantic the preparations of this enemy, Russia, were against the Reich and Europe. He said that the enemy does not consist of human beings but of animals or beasts. The enemy is fighting with a bestial lust for blood and out of cowardice and fear. But this enemy is already broken and will never rise again. Stalin said, "One death is a tragedy, a million, a statistic."

Anglo-American hopes of survival and ultimate victory depended, first of all, upon defense of the USSR. And second, only if Britain and America could launch a large scale offensive against the Axis in some other theater of war. It had to be an attack powerful enough to divert Nazi forces from the East so that the Soviet Union would be able to fight on and perhaps inflict on Hitler the fate of Napoleon. Whether Britain's shortages of men and arms and America's shortages of a will to fight could be overcome in time was uncertain in the third autumn of the war for the world.

Martin Olson

During 1939, Russia pursued the same course toward Nazism as Chamberlain did but with bitter results. There was a slight difference. The West praised Hitler early for saving Europe from Communism. Moscow praised Hitler late for fighting the Anglo-French. The Anglo-French appeasers sought safety by turning Hitler against Russia. The Moscow appeasers sought safety by turning Hitler against the Western powers. The British failed miserably. The Soviet foreign office succeeded well.

Successful appeasement is as fatal as an unsuccessful appeasement. For appeasement is seen as a weakness. France and Britain learned that later to the delight of the Fuhrer.

"Simple words, short maxims, homely truths, old sayings, are the masters of the world. In them is the hiding of the power that forms the character, controls conduct, and makes individuals and nations what they are. Great reformations, great revolutions in society, great eras in human progress and improvement, start from good words, right words, sound words, spoken in the fitting time, and finding their way to human hearts as easily as the birds find their homes."

D. March

CHAPTER SEVEN – THE UNITED STATES

" 'Now! Now!' cried the Queen. 'Faster! Faster!' And they went so fast that at last they seemed to skim through the air, hardly touching the ground with their feet, till suddenly, just as Alice was getting quite exhausted, they stopped, and she found herself sitting on the ground breathless and giddy. The Queen propped her up against a tree and said kindly, 'You may rest a little now.' Alice looked round her in great surprise. 'Why, I do believe we've been under this tree the whole time! Everything's just as it was!' 'Of course it is,' said the Queen: 'what would you have it?' 'Well, in our country,' said Alice, still panting a little, 'you'd generally get to somewhere else – if you ran very fast for a long time, as we've been doing.' 'A slow sort of country!' said the Queen. 'Now, here, you see, it takes all the running you can do, to keep in the same place. If you want to get somewhere else, you must run at least twice as fast as that!' "[1]

Fear of Communism on the part of people of property was high in the Western European democracies. Anglo-French isolationists tended to be political conservatives speaking for blue blood and large bank accounts, whereas proponents of collective security and world order were more frequently liberal or radical spokesmen for workers, peasants, and small businessmen. In America, big business was largely internationalist, whereas those who claimed to speak for urban workers, western farmers, and the lower middle class followed a tradition of liberalism, which was heavily charged with the fear of foreign entanglements.

Charges of dragging the country into war were hurled by Anglo-French aristocrats and industrialists against liberals and radicals, and by American liberals and radicals against arms manufacturers, Wall Street, and the international bankers. In France and Britain the politicians in power reflected the desires and prejudices of the moneyed elite, whereas the American New Deal aroused bitter resentment among businessmen, large and small.

Since the founding of America, the United States up until 1914 enjoyed isolationism. It was remote enough as to not get involved in any disputes occurring in Europe or Asia.

British capitalists had no desire to compete for power with the United States, but instead shared a common interest in preserving the world balance and keeping open the world channels of trade and investment.

The outbreak of hostilities between the two European coalitions in 1914 caused the United States to proclaim its neutrality as it had done in all European wars. An immensely profitable trade in munitions at once developed with the Allies. The effective Allied blockade of Germany prevented this trade from going to both sets of belligerents. The United States was willing to trade with anyone at this time. However, it leaned more and more toward the Allies, and this not for humanitarian or sentimental reasons expressed in war slogans, but for very tangible considerations connected with business and power politics. Allied defeat would probably mean Allied bankruptcy. American business had little to lose and everything to gain from Allied victory. A victory of the central powers would not only imperil these economic interests but would completely upset the balance of power and give Germany such a position of overwhelming preponderance on the Continent and throughout the world that even American security might eventually be endangered.

In addition, Germany was an autocracy and the Allies and the United States were democracies. Also, the U-boat blockade of the Allies endangered American lives. Germany was ruthless, lawless, uncivilized. The Allies were considerate, law-abiding, and virtuous. When Germany announced the resumption of unrestricted submarine warfare on February 1, 1917, President Woodrow Wilson severed diplomatic relations. On April 6, 1917, the United States declared war on Germany. A strengthened American Navy joined the Allied squadrons. Billions of dollars were raised and loaned to the Allied governments. Neutrality had failed to protect European interests and isolation was abandoned in favor of active participation in the European contest. Victory came in 1918 and the United States shared in the glory.

President Wilson had been a student of history. And he tried to convince his constituents to join the League of Nations but they refused. He then warned his countrymen that if they rejected the League, they would be obliged to fight another world war in twenty years. He also told them, "I would rather fail in an enterprise that I know must some day succeed than succeed in an enterprise that I know some day must fail." They paid no attention. They had already forgotten why they went to war. In their flight from responsibility, they wanted no one to remind them of the price of peace.

Following Wilson's exit from office in 1920, Warren Harding and Calvin Coolidge brought twelve consecutive years of Republican rule. Republican rule meant isolationism with a vengeance. Immigration was cut off and almost insurmountable tariff walls were erected. The Allies were required to sign on the dotted line for the repayment of their war debts.

During the 1920's the United States, as the wealthiest and most powerful of the great powers, helped to prevent the establishment of a viable world order to supercede the politics of power. Its tariff policies made impossible the payment of the war debts and insured the eventual loss of the billions of private capital, which flowed into European investments.

The Republican administrations made various gestures in the direction of peace, disarmament, and international cooperation. The United States participated in the General Disarmament Conference of the League of Nations and eloquently urged armament reduction, without being willing to commit itself to cooperation or even consultation with other powers in the interests of peace. In world politics, those who give no help to others against aggression are finally helpless themselves against aggression.

In 1932-1933, the full impact of the Great Depression paralyzed American business and finance. President Herbert Hoover and his party were swept from power by an impoverished and despairing electorate. Franklin D. Roosevelt, who promised reform, recovery and a New Deal for the forgotten man, entered the White House even as Adolf Hitler was establishing the Nazi dictatorship in the Reich.

This was a shift from Republicans to Democrats; one in which the administration of government was taken out of the hands of American big business and put into the hands of a new elite of liberal intellectuals who saw themselves not merely as the champions of workers, farmers and the lower middle class but as the builders of a new American dream.

The President, with his inherited wealth was detested as a traitor to his class by most Americans of means. Since he liked being liked, and feared being hated, he was ever tempted to shift his opinion, despite his desire to build a better American society and a free world order.

Lower posts in the Department of State and the Foreign Service were filled by professional diplomats rather then by deserving local politicians. The upper posts went chiefly to able career men or to prominent Democrats with money. Some of these men saw the world as it was and urged common action among the democracies to resist in time the rising tide of Fascism. Others were committed by prejudices of class or creed to appeasing the aggressors. A small but potent group of lesser bureaucrats saw the world as Hitler desired them to see it.

The chief obstacle in the way of a consistent American foreign policy after 1933 lay in the fact that most of the national legislators and many of the voters of the United States believed sincerely that safety and prosperity were to be had not by collaboration with other democratic nations but by scrupulous avoidance of all responsibilities, risks and entanglements. President Roosevelt and his immediate advisers knew better. But the art of politics in a democracy is the art of compromise. So firmly did the leaders of Britain, France and America believe in the principle of compromise during the years of the great retreat that they compromised all their principles in its name.

Widespread sentiment in favor of withdrawing diplomatic and military protection from American private interests abroad found expression in the good neighbor policy and in the neutrality legislation. Americans were in effect told that they were forbidden to make loans or to sell arms to countries at war.

The failure of disarmament led to intensified preparations for defense. The American Army, Navy and Air Force were enlarged even though in the first years of Franklin D. Roosevelt's first term most Americans permitted themselves to be persuaded that they could escape involvement in other people's quarrels by running away or by minding their own business or by abandoning business, which might drag them into war. This stance was eagerly endorsed by millions who wished to believe that war could be escaped by abandoning rights instead of enforcing them and for insulating America from a dangerous world rather than organizing the world for collective security.

War abroad had become inevitable. He result was a new American neutrality policy dictated by isolationists and designed not to facilitate American cooperation with the League States in preserving peace and restraining aggression, but to ensure American non-involvement in war when it should come. This would be impossible. The United States could not achieve isolation in a world in which Americans trade and investments were scattered over the five continents and the seven seas.

There was a double problem resulting from the arms trade and neutrality: both were linked together in a somewhat artificial fashion as private arms interests had repeatedly defied or circumvented governmental action designed to control the arms traffic; often promoted sales through bribery of foreign officials; employed American officials to secure contracts abroad; sold arms to both sides simultaneously in war; armed both factions in civil wars; stimulated armaments races; organized lobbies to oppose arms embargoes and to work for larger military and naval appropriations; reached agreements with foreign competitors for the division of markets and profits; and indulged in sundry other practices designed to enrich the merchants of death.

In keeping the United States at peace, it was generally assumed by Congress, the press, and the public that the United States becomes involved in war by virtue of damage to American interests resulting from hostilities among other states. Also, that Americans become involved in European wars by virtue of the plots of munitions makers, bankers, and exporters bent upon making blood money out of the world's problems and determined to make their own profits a national interest for which the United States must fight. In the third place, that the price of peace was the sacrifice of profits and that insurance against war was to be had by the abandonment of trade and investments abroad. Finally, that true neutrality implied complete impartiality between belligerents with no distinctions drawn between aggressors and victims of aggression. All these assumptions were partly or completely false and did not prevent them from being accepted and acted upon by those who preferred wishful thinking to a stern facing of facts.

On May 16, 1940, the President went before Congress to ask for a huge defense appropriation and a plane building capacity of 50,000 units per year. There was no notable dissent until Colorel Charles Lindburgh three days later demanded by radio that America "stop this hysterical chatter of calamity and invasion. No one wishes to attack us and no one is in a position to do so." Still, the majority of legislators and citizens, blinded by the fear of war, believed that America was in no danger or could somehow be defended after the arrival of an invader.

The President could either do nothing, apart from urging measures of defense, which he knew could never by themselves defend America, or he could exercise his executive discretion without regard for Congress. He chose the latter course.

On September 3, he arranged an agreement between the British Ambassador at Washington and the Secretary of State the right to lease naval and air bases in Newfoundland and in the islands of Bermuda, the Bahamas, Jamaica, St. Lucia, Trinidad and Antigua and in British Guiana. Congress was outflanked. Wendell Willkie, contender for the Presidency in the next election, endorsed the purpose of the agreement but found it regrettable that the President had not obtained prior approval from Congress.

Americans eagerly applauded the pledges of peace, which Roosevelt and Willkie both made in their bid for votes. The Republican Party declared its platform was "firmly opposed to involving this nation in foreign war. The Republican Party stands for Americanism, preparedness and peace." The Democratic platform said, "We will not participate in foreign wars, and we will not send our army, navy or air forces to fight in foreign lands outside of the Americas, except in the case of attack." "I give you the pledge," said Willkie, "No American soldier boy will be sent to the shambles of any European trench." "Your boys," declared Roosevelt, "are not going to be sent into any foreign war. The purpose of our defense is defense." Hitler gave silent cheers.

The Compulsory Military service and Training Law of September 16, 1940, introduced conscription for the first time during peace in the history of the Republic. The Two Ocean Navy bill of July 19 authorized a seventy percent increase in sea forces. Early in the new year the Navy was reorganized into an Atlantic squadron, a Pacific squadron and an Asiatic squadron in an unmistakable gesture of warning to Tokyo and the Axis.

Roosevelt further stated to Congress that the United States would come to the aid of any Allied country finding itself threatened by war. "We shall send you, in ever-increasing numbers, ships, planes, tanks, guns. This is our purpose and our pledge. In fulfillment of this purpose we will not be intimidated by the threats of dictators. In the future days, which we seek to make secure, we look forward to a world founded upon four essential human freedoms: The first is

105

freedom of speech and expression – everywhere in the world. The second is freedom of every person to worship God in his own way – everywhere in the world. The third is freedom from want – which, translated into world terms, means economic understandings which will secure to every nation a healthy peacetime life for its inhabitants – everywhere in the world. The fourth is freedom from fear – which, translated into world terms, means a world-wide reduction of armaments to such a point and in such a thorough fashion that no nation will be in a position to commit an act of physical aggression against any neighbor – anywhere in the world. Freedom means the supremacy of human rights everywhere."

This Act was signed by the President on March 11, 1941. The result was very strange. The American Government transferred money, arms and planes to Britain. The same American Government forbade American citizens, under heavy penalties, to lend money to Britain or to sell arms or planes on any basis. American goods were pledged to Britain, but American ships were forbidden to carry them and the American Navy was forbidden to insure the arrival of the goods.

Confusion was worse confounded in the Asiatic theater of war. For here the administration gave aid to the Chinese against Japan and simultaneously encouraged American sellers and shippers to give aid to Japan against China. Exports of scrap iron and steel were embargoed in 1940 but finished iron and steel were still sold freely to Japan in 1941. Aviation gasoline was embargoed in 1940 but other forms of gasoline and oil, from which aviation gasoline could be refined, were sold in ever greater amounts in the early months of 1941. Americans gave generously to aid the Chinese victims of Japanese bombs, which were dropped by planes made of American materials and flying on fuel sold by Americans.

After years of silence, the President explained why this was allowed. "It was very essential to prevent a war from starting in the South Pacific. If we had cut the oil off, the Japanese probably would have gone down to the Dutch East Indies." The wounded women and children of Chungking were therefore told that America had helped the Japanese to bomb them in order to keep the Japanese from bombing the rubber and tin of the East Indies, which America needed.

The noisy minority that did so much to confuse thought and paralyze action during the time of America's greatest peril consisted, as in other democracies, of diverse elements united only by their determination to oppose and obstruct. That the administration could make any headway at all against this chorus of defeatism was due to the fact that most Americans, for all their indecision, retained some vestiges of common sense. They feared and hated Hitler and all his works and insisted on all-out aid to Hitler's foes even at the risk of war.

The torpedoing in the South Atlantic on May 21 of the *Robin Moor*, first American vessel to be sunk by the Nazis, led to a sharp diplomatic protest to Berlin. This resulted in the freezing of all Axis funds in the United States, including the closing of all German consulates and the withdrawal for improper and unwarranted activities of the German Library of Information, the German Railway

Office and the Transocean News Service. Roosevelt called the Reich an international outlaw.

Iceland was struck next. President Roosevelt told Congress that Iceland was occupied by the Germans and "The United States cannot permit the occupation by Germany of strategic points in the Atlantic to be used as air or naval bases for eventual attack against the Western Hemisphere." A German seizure of Iceland would threaten Greenland and North America as well as North Atlantic shipping and the steady flow of munitions to Britain.

Despite moves made to protect American interests, North America was still disunited as World War II entered its third year. Few Americans favored active participation in hostilities. Few opposed aid to the Allies. But almost all were at war within themselves, for they desired the defeat of the Axis without desiring to pay any part of the price in struggle and pain. Most of them wanted victory without war.

By the approach of autumn of 1941, 2,000 Latin American firms and individuals were charged with aiding the Axis. The President froze their funds in the United States and froze all Japanese assets, restricted trade, and warned of worse to come when Japan moved into southern Indo-China. Arms and other supplies were given to Britain, dispatched to China on credit and sold to Russia for cash.

During this time, no American guns were fired, no American troops were ordered into action, no American planes attacked the enemy, no American ships of war sought out the foe on any sea. America was still at peace.

This strange state of affairs was not unprecedented. Hitler's Reich, Mussolini's Italy and Hirohito's Japan had been at peace for the better part of a decade while their leaders inspired their subjects with martial fervor, built up the greatest war machine of the ages, conquered China, Ethiopia, Spain, Austria, Czechoslovakia and Albania, and prepared the new world order.

The enemy leaders were too shrewd to provoke America into open war. And the leaders of America were too timid, too hopeful, too democratic, too politically minded to risk a plea to Congress for a declaration of war, or to wage actual war without declaring it.

In the face of dangers grown to terrifying proportions, the Americans of the 1940's were still so bent on pursuing pleasure and avoiding pain that they would risk nothing beyond their pocketbooks in what most of them still believed were other people's wars. This delusion would be fully dispelled only when the bombs should begin falling on their heads out of their own skies. By doing nothing, they would inevitably share the fate of other peoples similarly doomed to defeat and subjugation by their own irresponsibility.

Wars in our time are commonly lost long before the test of battle by the refusal of the losers to fight them until the hour of possible victory is past. In seeking victory without fighting Americans might well find themselves in the end alone, fighting without victory.

President Roosevelt's words and deeds during September showed evidence of a growing determination, in the White House if not in Congress, to do what was necessary before the hour for action had passed.

On Labor Day, 1941, the President asserted: "Our fundamental rights, including the rights of labor, are threatened by Hitler's violent attempt to rule the world. We cannot hesitate, we cannot equivocate, in the great task before us. Forces of insane violence have been let loose by Hitler upon this earth. We must do our full part in conquering them. There are a few appeasers and Nazi sympathizers who say it cannot be done. They even ask me to negotiate with Hitler, to pray for crumbs from his victorious table. They do, in fact, ask me to become the modern Benedict Arnold and betray all I hold dear. This course I have rejected. I reject it again. We shall do everything in our power to crush Hitler and his Nazi forces."

Three days later the destroyer *Greer*, en route to Iceland, was attacked by a Nazi submarine. It replied by dropping depth charges. The President ordered the navy to track down and eliminate the attacker. In the waters between Iceland and Greenland three merchant vessels, all of United States ownership and Panamanian registry, were torpedoed: the *Sessa* on August 17, the *Montana* on September 11, and the *Pink Star* on September 19. Five days later a shoot first order went into effect. American opinion approved but a large segment of the population continued to demand peace.

Great nations unwilling to face their destiny have no future. If America continued to close its eyes and minds, the Nazi Reich would rule the world.

On June 22, 1941, Hitler attacked Russia from the Arctic Circle to the Black Sea. On December 6, 1941, a hundred Soviet divisions counter-attacked in forty degrees below zero weather and threw back the Nazi invaders.

On December 7, 1941, Japan attacked Pearl Harbor. American Marines landed on Guadalcanal on August 7, 1942. The Soviet forces crushed the Germans at Stalingrad on January 30, 1943. The Western Allies entered Rome on June 4, 1944, and landed at Normandy on June 6, 1944.

On April 12, 1944, Franklin Delano Roosevelt, President of the United States, died. Harry S. Truman, Vice-president became President. When Truman was told to come over to the White House immediately, and to enter by way of the main Pennsylvania Avenue entrance, Truman said under his breath, "Jesus Christ and General Jackson." He asked Mrs. Roosevelt, "Is there anything I can do?" She responded with, "No. For you are the one in trouble now."

Following World War II and the battle with Japan, General Douglas MacArthur was instructed to assist the Japanese with the work of reparation. In that effort, the United States agreed to loan Japan six-hundred million dollars and would take in security notes from Japan to that effect. The Swiss Trust was to become the depository for those notes. These notes were known as the MacArthur Fund Notes.

What took place next turned the course of history. The attorney representing Japan in the United States was Richard Nixon, who got the position from Thomas Dewey who had been the attorney representing Japan in the US. And he had an ulterior motive in playing this role. He approached the Japanese business people and the administration in the years following this loan and made the deal of the century. He advised them that he would soon be running for Vice-president under General Dwight Eisenhower and in time was planning to run for the office of President. He made an agreement with Japan that, in return for some monetary support, he would make the MacArthur Fund Notes disappear. Japan readily agreed. Those notes today would be worth over a trillion dollars. Nixon sold out his country in return for the position of President.

Richard Nixon made a statement in 1973 in which he said, "I made my mistakes, but in all my years of public life, I have never profited from public service. I earned every cent. And in all my years in public life, I have never obstructed justice. I welcome this kind of examination because people have got to know whether or not their President is a crook. Well, I am not a crook."

Now one must remember, Nixon was a lawyer. Also, his work with Japan was before he became President. So, his statement about his public service was technically correct, but not morally correct.

Before Mihaly, as Chairman of the Swiss Trust, and the members of the Trust would accept the Japanese Secret MacArthur Notes, they had an extensive investigation made on the background and history of the notes as well as what Vice-president Nixon did with the notes. They had to be sure of their authenticity before Mihaly accepted the role of managing the notes. The Doctor knew of the dangers associated with these notes so he had a report made and filed in Brussels, Belgium with such specifics included as to what should become of them if he were to die or be killed. Such a death would trigger the report to be released to the proper authorities.

I worked for the Chairman of the Trust as well as Prudential at that time. I received a call from the Chairman the first week of January, 1989, explaining in some detail that the Trust controlled vast sums of Japanese government-backed CD's. He further stated that he wanted to implement these CD's into a program using US Government guarantees as insurance for some third-world projects that in the end would result in taxes payable to the US Government and aid in the reduction of the US deficit. He then sent an overview letter of the program to me. It briefly outlined that the Trust filed five-billion US dollars equal in Japanese yen in 1986 with the US Customs Department in Washington. The reason the Trust did this was to prove to US officials that there were certain Japanese notes that did exist, contrary to what the United States had been vehemently claiming over the years as to their non-existence, and that the Chairman could bring some of these notes into the United States as evidence. I will explain more about this later.

The Trust, through Japanese Nationals who worked directly with the Minister of Finance and the Central Bank, would be working in concert with these people to develop this transaction by using these CD's, or securities, so that they might not upset the International Money Market. Since these securities were private there was no requirement to file with the Securities Exchange Commission. An additional problem would be to operate with the large amount of cash on the Currency Exchange International Market, which could trigger again undesirable shifting concerning the Yen/Dollar exchange rate and would provoke intervention by various central banks in order to keep the equilibrium under control.

The Chairman wanted me to go to Washington and meet government officials to discuss the Japanese securities, which, with what little detailed information I had, could be tricky and very dangerous. It was like going into a lion's den. One other thought plagued me, *Why me, when the doctor has lawyers available to do the task?*

Now that I know the Chairman better and his use of caution in all his dealings he probably asked me because he knew that I would not misuse the information I had become privy to for personal gain and that I would tell him honestly about any reaction from Washington.

So, armed with what little I had to go on, at the request of the Chairman and with a copy of the Chairman's instructions as well as a letter explaining what I knew about this subject, I called Chief of Staff Governor John Sununu's office to obtain the name of the proper person to contact. This was followed by a call to US Treasury Secretary Brady's office who referred me to a Don Chiodo who referred me to Meg Lundsager, Director of International Affairs, who further referred me to Department of Commerce Secretary Designate, Robert Mosbacker, and then finally to the White House. I called the White House to verify that they had received a copy of the Chairman's letter but was responded to in the negative.

The next day I called the State Department, Japanese Desk, and they advised that they also never received the letter. So, I called the White House again and they gave me the number for the Central Control Center between the White House and the State Department. This way I could check on things by myself. I called and the young lady went through with me the documents that passed that day; she could not find any letter. So much for tight security and communications in Washington. I did all the above by telephone, letter or fax up to this point.

I called again, at the request of the Chairman to the State Department, Japanese Desk Officer William Breer, on the first of April 1989 to make an appointment to see him on the nineteenth of that month. When the day arrived, I drove from New Hampshire to DC. Being very familiar with the area, I knew exactly where to go. My meeting with Bill Breer lasted an hour. I covered all the points that were sent to Secretary Brady, the White House, and Secretary Mosbacker. I remained overnight at a Virginia motel so that I could stop by and try to see Secretary Brady or Meg Lundsager at the office of the US Treasury the following day. I did not realize that stopping by the Treasury to see these people was like asking for an audience with the Pope. It was almost like going through blood tests, x-rays and urinalyses to get in. I was asked by Lundsager's secretary if I minded stopping by their office on G Street to discuss the subject with the officials there. So I trotted over to G Street, ninth floor, as a lamb to the slaughter.

After I passed an armed guard behind a bullet-proof window, I immediately met up with two men who politely asked me to step into a room off the corridor I just came through. A third man was waiting inside the room. They began a series of questions posed to me but very obviously dealing with what I knew to be the contents of the letter from the Chairman. It began with their asking me for my reason in wanting to meet Brady or Lundsager.

"Look! Let me tell you this one final time," I began. "What I know about these Japanese notes is that they were entrusted to the Swiss Trust. They were a political hot potato to the Japanese for the reasons I already explained. They wanted them deposited somewhere so they gave them to the Trust to hold. A few leaked out and ended up somehow in Las Vegas. I don't know how; that happened before I came on board. People who got them got arrested. Nothing was ever done with the notes.

"The only activity will be the sixteen or seventeen billion dollars worth that will be coming into the country and that I was to act as a courier to take them back to Tokyo, Japan. If there's a problem with that or for some reason that goes against US policy, let me know and I'll refuse the job."

I was very uncomfortable especially after having been truthful in telling them everything I knew. I had no idea what else they had in mind and just their methods of bullying me the way that they did made me very nervous. I fully believed they could read this in my body language and that is why they were relentless in trying to discover some information I might have inadvertently forgot to mention. What they failed to understand was that the Trust would never have allowed me full knowledge, only some, and that was on a need to know basis.

If they wanted anything more, they would have to ask the Chairman himself. I could offer only what I knew at that point. I could see by their questions that they were trying to set me up to report to them on the Chairman and about the securities on a regular basis. I had no problem with this. As I said earlier, I am a devoted American and I believe in my country. My work was on the up and up and I did nothing to be ashamed of. My only concern was in accomplishing what the Chairman had sent me to Washington to do without jeopardizing my credibility.

Eventually the man in charge came in and said, "Look, we know that Dr. Mihaly will come through and deliver so you should stay with the Chairman." What he was saying was that he knew more about these Japanese notes than even I did at that time and it, therefore, was in both of our best interests that I remain close to the doctor. Somehow, even without my telling them, they also knew that I did all of the Chairman's research on developments and they wanted me to report to them regularly.

The sixteen-billion US dollars equivalent yen as told to the Secret Service was moved from Japan to Los Angeles by the Chairman's British courier. The Secret Service called me two weeks later to confirm that move.

The Japanese notes were at the very heart of this entire scenario. I alluded to them earlier so it is important that I explain here exactly what they entailed and what knowledge I had of them.

Following World War II and the battle with Japan, Foreign Minister Shgemitsu Mamoru in representing Japan signed the unconditional surrender documents with General Douglas MacArthur representing the United States and its allies. This took place on September 2, 1945. General MacArthur, the supreme commander of Japan's occupation forces, began immediately to carry out the policies set forth in his instructions from President Harry Truman. His instructions were to disarm, demilitarize and return overseas portions of Japan's empire to its former owners; those properties taken by Japan as a result of its invasions. General MacArthur was to remove any and all obstacles for development of a democratic society and foster a free economy for an adequate peaceful existence. The General decided that Japan should retain its own government for routine administration and help execute orders from the Supreme Commander for Allied Powers, known as SCAP. It was at this point in time that a man named Shibusawa Keizo was the Finance Minister and an officer and large shareholder in numerous Zaibatsu controlled companies including the Teikoku Bank of Japan. In order to understand what this means, it is important that the term 'Zaibatsu' be explained.

Japan and the United States are two totally different cultures that share the same basic problem of greed, which is a common thread throughout the world. Japan, with its ancient culture, emphasizes its basis to have a closed society versus the young American culture that retains as its basis an open society. The common thread between the two countries is not only greed but control as well. Japan controls its society through secret societies known as Zaibatsu and also through the discipline of the Japanese people. The United States controls its society through its political leaders, banking and industrial leaders, and the limited knowledge allowed to be exposed to their society. The average US citizen does not have any interest in global topics as we have had no internal wars since the Civil War and have had things pretty much our way since the 1950's. The Japanese have had it well only since the 1950's and have had only growth in the country at the expense of its hard-working people.

On September 22, 1945, SCAP decreed orders to break up the Zaibatsu and prevent their revival. This meant the break-up of the four largest companies: Mitsui, Mitsubishi, Sumitomo and Yasuda. Zaibatsu leaders, not given a chance to cultivate influence with SCAP, devised a plan to save their companies. Many went into partnership with American businessmen and lawyers, most of whom became millionaires or billionaires and live in Japan even to the present time.

MacArthur vowed to break up the Zaibatsu and at the same time the Chinese Nationalists along with the Australians, the British and the USSR demanded Japanese factories as reparation for their losses during the war. If they succeeded, Japan's industry would be destroyed. MacArthur announced that there would be no reparations but that the US would provide assistance. Operating under their new constitution, and backed by the aid of America, the Japanese people saved their political and economic system, the same one that had been in use in prewar Japan.

Although the Zaibatsu were no longer as powerful as they once had been, they still had strong allies in the United States. Leading American banks and corporations had capital and business ties of long standing with Japanese firms. American creditors and investors who had significant sums of money wrapped up in Japanese firms were anxious to recover their investments. Some four-hundred million dollars were outstanding, including interest and dividends and overdue licensing fees. These creditors were lobbying vigorously in Washington against Japanese reform. They wanted to protect their investments as well as any future investments.

In an effort to appease these creditors and to encourage the rebuilding of Japan, Under-Secretary of the Army, William H. Draper, was sent to Japan to initiate changes in policy. Accompanying Draper on this adventure was Percy H. Johnson, Chairman of Chemical Bank and Trust of New York, which had close ties with the Mitsui Bank, one of the four Zaibatsu conglomerates. There would be a continuation of business between the corporations with interests in Japan and the Japanese people. In addition to this, by the end of the year 1948, the US provided four-hundred billion dollars in aid to Japan to help rebuild and bolster its economy. This money transaction was not made public to the American people for two reasons: first, because of the pressure put onto President Truman by the moguls of Wall Street who were teetering on the verge of some gigantic losses with the investments they made in Japan before the war; and second, to a lesser degree, because of the feelings of ill will by the rest of America toward Japan as a result of the war. This deal with Japan was made clandestinely and it was to remain a secret forever. The belief was that the money, along with its accompanying interest, would eventually over time be returned to the United States.

For Japan this was a good investment. During the 1960's their exports rose seventeen percent a year. With Japan's favorable balance of trade, which averaged less than four-hundred million dollars a year since 1960, this multiplied to an average of better than two-billion dollars a year between 1967 and 1970 and nearly eight-billion dollars in 1971. This changed Japan from a debtor nation to a creditor nation and one of the world's biggest international lenders and investors.

This secret investment was a loan to Japan and was to be repaid with interest over a period of years. In receipt for the loan, documents known as securities or notes were printed to be given to the United States as paper collateral. The moneys transferred to the Japanese government for this purpose were to be known as the MacArthur Funds.

To return to where I was before my explanation of the loan for the renaissance of Japan known as the MacArthur Funds, I was held in this detention area at the Treasury Office for about three hours. In an effort to prove to them that I had no intention of leaving the States and disappearing because of the huge amount of money represented by these Japanese notes and the fact that I had a relationship with the doctor who held them, I offered to give them my passport.

"My allegiance is to the United States," I reminded them, "and I have no desire to do anything that would jeopardize my country. If it makes you feel any better, why don't you just take my passport as proof that I mean what I say?"

"No, that's not necessary," one of them finally answered. "Besides that, if you are to report to us concerning your work with the doctor, you will need that for your travels, especially if you are to deliver those notes to Japan."

I was then escorted to my car in the parking garage below the Treasury building and never did meet with either of the two people I had intended to see.

I drove out of Washington that afternoon and returned to New Hampshire. I had no idea what might transpire over the next few days. I went back to work at Prudential. In no time at all, a call was received by Prudential from the Secret Service. They were checking up on me. No one in the company asked any questions, but the curiosity level was high as people tried to listen as they wondered what was going on.

The Chairman called me the next day to ask me to arrange with the State Department Japanese Desk, Bill Breer, to accept a call from the doctor's Japanese law firm in Tokyo. Upon completing this request, I discovered that within three months Bill Breer was transferred to Tokyo, no doubt as a result of the Secret Service trying to keep track of the MacArthur Funds. It was obvious that something bigger than what I had already thought was big was occurring. Everything was on a need to know basis.

Up until this time, I truthfully had very little information concerning these Japanese securities. When the Chairman returned to Florida from California after spending time going back and forth on several occasions, he explained to me in some detail but not all—about the source of these securities and how they came under control of the Trust and the Chairman. He then stressed the importance of developing a detailed program to handle major overseas projects to be controlled from United States soil.

Dr. Mihaly told me that the CD's started out as redemption bonds issued by the Japanese Government. About two percent of them are still in circulation today. The rest were exchanged for certificates of deposit. These CD's, carrying a nominal interest rate, cannot be cashed in or used as collateral without approval from Japan's Minister of Finance. When the Dai-Ichi Kangyo Bank redeemed the bonds and issued CD's in place of them, they totaled approximately 600 billion US dollars equal yen. That was twice the value of the bank. The bank then gave these Japanese CD's, which are really the property of the Japanese Government as all banks are under control of the government, to Japanese Nationals who embarked on a search for someone to take control of them as there was nothing the Nationals could do with them otherwise. A more pressing reason was the fact that some of these secret notes found their way out of the hands of the Nationals and several of these people were killed as a result—some, obviously, by forced suicide. Because the notes represented such a large amount of money, possessing them was dangerous; one literally took one's life in his own hands. After realizing this, the balance of the Nationals looked for someone to take control of the notes. They turned to Switzerland and ended up with the Chairman of the Swiss Trust. The Swiss Trust was a depository for the very wealthy. They never did anything with the money before the First World War. It was managed by Dr. Mihaly's father and there was no real name given to the Trust other than just being known as the Swiss Trust. It must be said at this point that the Swiss do not trust anybody; everything is secretive. A good reason as well why they were the perfect depository for the secret MacArthur Funds. If it were not for my dealings with the World Bank, I might not have gotten to know Dr. Mihaly to the degree that I did. His family was all blue-blood going back to the Hungarian monarchy.

After reviewing all the doctor's reports and coming to an understanding of the securities, its history and its purpose, I realized the value they held intrinsically and how important it was for the United States to benefit from them. These CD's over the years have been controlled and grossly abused by high officials of the government of Japan, a number of whom have corruptly utilized very large sums of money from the fund for their own personal gain.

Once the notes were placed with the Swiss Trust, the Chairman formulated a plan that would convert them into CD's and by that process would give them true, rather than just paper, value. The problem was that this entire process was a secret and was to remain a secret. No moneys and no interest income were ever returned to the United States as repayment. Because of the maneuvering between President Truman, trying to help the whores of

Wall Street, and the concern by General Douglas MacArthur trying to assist Japan in rebuilding, the US Secret Service was employed to go to great lengths to conceal these notes and their original source. Above all, they wanted to take possession of the notes so that they could be destroyed and no one in the United States would be the wiser. [6]

The best way to explain how our country's leaders can pull off these types of secret negotiations is to come to an understanding of the Washington mentality. To do that, I just need to give a brief introduction to a Washington insider.

I met with Clark Clifford several times in, as well as outside of, his office. Clark was a smooth lawyer who had a very calm disposition, at least when I was with him. In addition to being an advisor to six Presidents, he also, for a short time, moved over to the Pentagon to become Secretary of Defense.

During my meetings with him regarding buying land for Sears because I had been for several years the contractor for new properties with that company, we had discussions concerning Washington and its politicians as well as the future of the District of Columbia and the United States. He told me his opinion regarding two subjects and that opinion has always stayed with me. The first was that the politicians and personnel inside the Washington Beltway feel that they are the United States, and all people outside the Beltway are servants who supply all their needs. The second was that he seriously felt that the present system of government would not last. I asked him why he thought that and how long he thought that period would be. He stated

125

that he did not know the length of time, only that it was destined to failure because it is riddled with decay and greed. Of all people, Clark should know because he worked most of his life inside the Beltway.

This reminds me of the volumes of history that comprise the decline and fall of the Roman Empire by Edward Gibbon (1776-1788) and his general observation on what happened to that great domain. The decline was the natural and inevitable effect of immoderate greatness in which prosperity ripened the principle of decay wherein the fabric of the government yielded to the pressure of its own weight.[3]

It is no surprise to hear some historians claim that scandal followed the introduction of Christianity and abuses took place, which had some influence on the fall. The Romans were ignorant of the extent of the danger that existed around them and the number of enemies who hated them. Danger came to them from an obscure people, the Arabs, who spread their conquests from India to Spain. These people had languished in poverty and contempt until a feeling of enthusiasm was breathed into their bodies and souls during the first century. It took 800 years for the Roman Empire to fall. Gibbon felt that a revolution such as that suffered by Rome could never happen again because Europe was divided into well-ordered independent states and kingdoms. He was convinced in his optimistic belief that there would be a continued progress for the civilized world.

Now comes the twenty-first century in which we have lightning speed for everything including all aspects of our lives. This lightning speed has only existed for the last forty or so years and is growing faster every year.

I am fascinated with history, more so from what I have experienced over the span of my lifetime. I lived through these past forty years and have seen some amazing things take place – both good and bad. My wife says that it is a waste of time writing about what was said or done so many years ago, especially that which involved President Richard Nixon because most people do not care. They are only interested in what is happening now. And the same people have developed an attitude that some of the stories from the past cannot occur again and cannot take place here. Some go so far as to not believe that such atrocities had really ever taken place. The old adage that one who does not study history is destined to repeat it can be seen as very evident in this current age of ours.

Teddy Roosevelt once said that the biggest problem in America is that we have too much tenacity. We never will be liked in the world because of this difficulty so we will even be hated.

I was reluctant to tell about Clark Clifford's feelings due to the government's actions regarding Doctor Mihaly and the Japanese Notes. Washington likes to keep secrets and respond only on a need to inform basis as far as the public taxpayer is concerned.

Once the Doctor made the decision to accept his role, he would proceed even in the face of great personal risk or death. He was not afraid. Of course, time took its toll. The US Secret Service and the Justice System made sure that the Doctor did not disclose any details of the notes or their connection to Richard Nixon. It finally did him in and he passed away.

The Doctor was, deep down, religious even though his scientific background demanded that every point was to be proven. He knew that only his faith would carry him. He always stated to me that he and I had a destiny and that was to fulfill the building of a medical university. Everything else he had been a part of, every project he had undertaken, was only a method to accomplish that destiny. Maybe some day someone will. But I feel that right now the only subject to be completed is Nixon's responsibility for the part he played in history.

On to the next conflict.

The peace was harder to win than the war.

In March, 1946, Churchill announced the descent of the Iron Curtain by Russia across Europe. Peace was a long way off.

After the war, barbarism and hatred seemed an uncontrollable genie unwilling to get back in its bottle.

KOREA

In 1910, Japan annexed Korea and ruled it until the end of World War II, after Japan lost the war. At that time, Korea was divided into two parts. The northern part would be known as the Democratic People's Republic of Korea and would be operated by the Soviet Union and its allies. The southern part would be known as the

Republic of Korea and would become independent with its own constitution but with assistance from the United States and its allies.

In August of 1947, China, Great Britain and the United States recommended a plan to reunify the country into one entity. However, Stalin and the USSR refused to cooperate. At this time, two events took place: first, the United States stopped any governmental authority in South Korea; and second, Kim Il Sung was made the leader of North Korea and claimed jurisdiction over the entire Korean Peninsula, which included the South.

The Koreans followed Japan's example to create her own industrial revolution but was delayed in its inception by frustration and imperfection in the quality of its products. The Japanese occupiers of Korea were followed by Russians and then Americans who installed hostile regimes based upon their own spheres of thinking. This was a move that would never work because the Orientals of that section of Asia had practiced their own way of thinking, which had been instilled in their people for millennia, and that mind-set was not to be easily changed, especially by outsiders. The North would be influenced by the Union of Soviet Socialist Republics and the South by the United States. The South was cut off from the sources of energy in the North and the North barricaded itself against the capitalism of the South. Both halves endured repressive regimes, which upheld traditional Korean distinction. The North continued to be under the rigid control of the USSR while the South met the more flexible authority of the United States. The populace, over the years, were led to believe that government is boss and the people inferior. The North wasted resources on heavy machinery paying little or no attention to the needs of the masses, while the South ruled by the old dynasty customs in which there was greater concern for the people and less emphasis on things.

The resulting Korean Conflict of 1950 to 1953 began as a consequence of the influence of these two factions. The Conflict was destructive and indecisive as the outside aid sponsors rolled back and forth. On occasion, American aid to the South stopped. The war was only suspended, never terminated. The cost of the country's defenses took all of the funds, depriving both sides of taking any advantage of any Asian reconstruction. The South would lose US money and the North could not get any much-needed industry to build within its borders. The miracle on the Han River, whereby Korea enjoyed great industrial expansion, was delayed until the 1960's when a new president named Park Chung Hee, took office. He launched a far right policy that assured success for the country and by the 1980's the gross national product per capita in South Korea was coming close to European levels.

At 4:00 a.m., Sunday morning, on June 25, 1950, North Korean soldiers crossed the 38th Parallel in a full-scale invasion of South Korea. Once informed of this invasion, the United Nations Security Council immediately passed a resolution calling on the Democratic People's Republic of Korea to cease hostilities and to withdraw. When the North Koreans refused, the Security Council passed a second resolution recommending that UN members furnish such assistance to the Republic of Korea as may be necessary to repel the armed attack and restore peace and security to the country. However, North Korea's forces were moving rapidly into the South capturing its capitol, Seoul. This event challenged the administration of President Harry Truman and the allies of the United States because if it went without a serious response, it would set a precedent that could easily undermine the confidence of post-World War II countries and their reliance on the United States for protection.

In 1950, Korea was a relatively small country with a population of about 30 million people. It was situated at a point surrounded by three great Asian nations: Japan, China, and the Soviet Union. Although it did not have any strategic advantage at this time, in later years it would prove to be critical to the security of the United States.

Over the years since its split, there had been numerous skirmishes in which the North Koreans clashed with the South. However, no one expected the invasion that took place in June of 1950. Wanting to remain uninvolved, the Truman Administration hesitated to act upon the invasion unless it was requested by the government of South Korea. Almost immediately, that request came and the President ordered General Douglas MacArthur to send in combat troops. Truman advised the American public of his intention to intervene. This was welcome news to the South Koreans but it was only a first step and the people of that Republic wanted more. America was not prepared, either by means of personnel or facilities, to support an armed conflict in that country.

It was perhaps good planning and training that gave the United States the advantage. By September, the US military managed to hold North Korea in check and to gain back for South Korea the control of Seoul.

The sustained heavy equipment losses to the North were substantial but the conflict was far from over. In late November, 1950, US Marines and infantry, fighting in bitterly cold weather conditions, found themselves in serious trouble. They were surrounded by a large armed group of Chinese Communists. Unsuccessful in their attempt to escape, many Marines were killed and only a few survived with frostbite. The growing Chinese forces crossed the 38th Parallel into South Korean territory.

One of the worst battles of the conflict came about as the result of a stalemate in which the two conflicting sides neither won any fight nor any territory. It was an area called Heartbreak Ridge and began with an attack on September 13, 1951. For two weeks, the claim of who won the mountaintop volleyed back and forth between ally and enemy. In every clash, troops were worn down from a beginning of bombs and bullets to that of grenades, bayonets and hand-to-hand fighting; and further worn down by physical exhaustion. Were it not for a battalion of armored tanks roaring up the mountain to reinforce allied positions, the fighting might have been won by the enemy. On October 13, French soldiers captured the last remaining Communist soldiers. Thousands of men had been killed or injured. The heaviest losses were sustained by the enemy; 25,000 dead or injured, compared to 3700 allied troops. Overall, United Nations troops and enemy troops in total sustained more than 40,000 casualties over this one piece of ground. With the United Nations Command taking the offensive and refusing to back down, it became obvious to the North Koreans and its allies that more losses were to be expected if the fighting continued. That understanding finally brought both factions back to the bargaining table.

Syngman Rhee, who had lived for decades in the United States, became the leader of South Korea at the time of the Conflict over the dividing line at the 38th Parallel. His administration had been accused of using the war to an even greater advantage for his country. The conspiracy theory was that he needed to suck in North Korea by making it appear that they were invading South Korea so that he could remain in power as well as to secure more aid from the United States to cover his massive domestic intelligence activities that had been surveilling North Korea. An appropriation brought before Congress was defeated in January of 1950 but the above reasoning was all Rhee needed as an excuse to receive significant aid from America. A conflict that started at the 38th parallel ended three years later at the 38th parallel. It was an undeclared conflict that never terminated.

Korea, the American forgotten war, was directed by General Douglas MacArthur who stated that, "This is my war." It ended the General's long war record by his being fired by the President of the United States. The Korean War was the first time that American troops faced Russian and Chinese troops. This was a war that claimed approximately 30,000 lives; some 6000 soldiers remained missing in action, and approximately two million lives in total were lost in the conflict. [4]

After MacArthur was fired and returned back to the United States, he made a speech to the National Association of Manufacturers where he stated that he knew how to end the Korean Conflict. MacArthur outlined his plan directly to Eisenhower, President elect, and to his Secretary of State designate, John Foster Dulles, as follows: Deliver an ultimatum to the Chinese to pull out of Korea or their cities would be bombed and their industrial bases wiped out. The Air Force would drop nuclear waste across North Korea, which would make it impossible for the Chinese to supply their 300,000 men in Korea any aid and impossible for those soldiers to get out; they would be trapped. They could also make an amphibious assault against the east and west coasts of North Korea while UN troops would move north of the 38th parallel. Eisenhower completely dismissed MacArthur's ideas as totally infeasible and disregarded the plan.

Today, North Korea possesses nuclear weapons capable of mass destruction. The fact that some of these weapons have been tested and portions of their shells have been found in Alaska means that the United States is now vulnerable to attack. In addition, that country is more than suspect in its research into biological weapons of mass destruction. UN soldiers continue to guard the border between North and South Korea in that area known as the demilitarized zone, established in July, 1953, with US military filling most of the slots for the UN.

Kim Il Sung came to power in 1946 while Stalin still was the leader of the USSR. He was regarded as the Great Father of the people of North Korea. The term father being construed to mean one who is deserving of love and reverence. His philosophy, put into practice in 1955, applied Marxism-Leninism, the living of one's life in a totally self-reliant country, which is totally loyal to the country's leader, to North Korean society. When he passed away in the early 1990's, his son, Kim Jung Il took control of the country. Currently, he is an even greater threat to the world than his father had been. He is making no apology for the fact that he is building, in opposition to a previous UN resolution for no nuclear arms, nuclear weapons that are capable of tremendous mass destruction and casualties.

A truly mad, mad world. No wonder the world has constant conflicts and wars. It resolves nothing, only creating more disasters.

VIETNAM

In July, 1885, the young, 13 year-old emperor, Ham Nghi fled Hue for the security of the mountains of central Vietnam. This is when the Vietnamese resistance to French colonial rule began. The decision to resist the imposition of the French protectorate was sudden, but not unplanned. Ham Nghi started for a mountain retreat that was supplied with food, ammunition and gold.

As a follower of Confucius, Nghi accepted his role as emperor by taking upon himself the full blame for the terrible things that had

135

transpired in his country but he also demanded that his people pay strict obedience to the monarchy and also to display complete hatred of the French.

As the French kept up their pursuit of Nghi, those who were the followers of Nghi were unable to reach their retreat. By-passing what was believed to be a safe haven, they went further into the remote mountains leaving the supplies of the retreat to the French enemies. Now Nghi and his people had to depend upon the support of small villages to exist.

Fortunately for Nghi, Vietnamese ambushes prevented French troops from easy access up to and through the mountains. These unique ambushes became the beginning of true guerrilla warfare.

Even with all the help he received and with all his careful traipsing through the brush, in November of 1888, Nghi was captured. He was exiled to the French colony in Algeria where he remained for the rest of his life.

By 1897, the last of the guerrilla forces in the Vietnamese mountains had been subdued. This began a decade of peace in which the French started the process of developing the new possessions they had conquered.

Had Nghi not been such an adamant follower of Confucius, he would have perhaps been able to succeed in his revolt against the French; however, Confucianism was limited in its teachings and philosophy. Its basis of loyalty to the family provided the enemy with a means by which it could extract information from the people it attacked. The French would arrest and threaten death to the parents of resistance fighters and, although that was a cruel tactic, it worked.

Over time, those who participated in defending Vietnam from the French would tell stories of the battles to their children. By 1903, these young men began plotting their means for independence, which was their goal. They saw how the Japanese were victorious over the Russian empire and that was proof that an Asian country could defeat a western power. This knowledge stimulated the next generation of Vietnamese resistance. Out of this period came two young leaders: Phan Boi Chan and Phan Chu Trinh.

In 1905, one of these men, Phan Boi Chan, sailed for Japan looking for Japanese support. He was disappointed when he found that Japan ruled out military aid. Instead, they suggested that the boy raise money to send young Vietnamese to Japan for advanced study in both military arts and modern technology.

Returning to Vietnam, Phan Boi Chan organized the 'Exodus to the East,' as the program to encourage study in Japan was called. By the summer of 1908, two-hundred young Vietnamese were studying in Japan.

By late 1907, the time was ripe for an attempt to force the French out of Vietnam. A plan was made in which the French officers of the Hanoi garrison would be poisoned by low-ranking native troops, who would then seize crucial points in the capitol.

Somehow, the French had sensed trouble and the plot was thwarted. Scores of rebels were sent to prison.

With the outbreak of World War I in 1914, another generation of Vietnamese resistance leaders had all but disappeared. Still, the Vietnamese people did not give up hope. It was not until 29-year old Nguyen Ai Quoc, a Vietnamese patriot, presented a petition in Paris for Vietnamese independence to the Versailles Peace Conference as decisions were being made for postwar Europe, that things turned worse. Paris quickly dismissed the petition striking another blow to independence for Vietnam.

Following World War I, especially in the years 1925 and 1926, agitation over the French control of Vietnam arose once again. In November, 1925, Alexandre Varenne came to Saigon as the new governor general for Indochina. He had been appointed by the leftist coalition that had just won the French elections. The Constitutionalists gave him a list of demands in which greater political rights for the people of Vietnam was primary. This was followed by a further demand that the Vietnamese be given assistance in the development of their economic and cultural life.

The Constitutionalists were looking for a harmonic relationship between the French and the Vietnamese but that proved to be a fatal mistake. Vietnam wanted nothing to do with the French. The Constitutional Party had lost their power and the French applauded that loss.

On Christmas Eve in 1927, a small group of anti-colonialists held a secret meeting in Hanoi. Here they established the Vietnamese Nationalist Party, modeled after the Kuomintang of China, the party of Chiang Kai-shek. This was to be the first revolutionary organization in Vietnam. It adopted Lenin's successful organizational principles in which a central committee issued orders that flowed downward to all echelons. They further organized into small cells, which would lessen the chance of detection by the French police.

According to the French Secret Police, the party grew rapidly to just under 2000 members divided among 120 cells. It drew its membership from those who did not fit the profile of the wealthy or the elite. Many of the members were students, small merchants or landlords.

The French police being wary of activities in Vietnam and realizing their continuing unpopularity, infiltrated the groups and before long had made numerous arrests destroying the party.

In August of 1938, the French government appointed General Georges Catroux as the governor general of Indochina. While France itself was occupied with the activities of Germany's Nazis, General Catroux was more concerned with the Japanese who had invaded China just the year previous and were still embroiled in battle there. The capture of Canton in 1938 and the Island of Hainan in 1939 brought Japan to Vietnam's border. The Japanese had been convinced that the fact they were unable to subdue China was because supplies were being carried to the Chinese military over the highways and railroads of Vietnam.

In 1939, when France entered World War II against Japan's ally, Nazi Germany, the Japanese began a propaganda and diplomatic campaign against this French connection to the Chinese government. However, as long as the French government remained steadfast, the

Japanese were unwilling to risk a war in Indochina because they realized what they could gain if France were to succumb to Germany.

The activities in Europe provided the Japanese a great opportunity in Southeast Asia. Immediately following the signing of the French-German armistice in June of 1940, the Japanese began a demand that France stop supplying the Chinese with war materials by way of Vietnam. Japan further sent a diplomatic mission to Germany to gain support for this demand. In quick time, General Catroux was notified that, should he continue to be the passageway between France and China, he would receive no military aid from England or the United States. Faced with this decision, he promised to cut the supply lines between Vietnam and China. Japan had another victory as a result of this move. But this was only the beginning.

Within days, Japan's troops poured south across the Chinese border into Vietnam. In three days the French resistance was crushed. There was no way the French could defeat the Japanese in Indochina. Japan established air bases there and began to garrison troops in Vietnam.

In the winter of 1940, the Japanese tried to entice Thailand to invade French Indochina in the area of Cambodia. The Thai government was only too willing to listen as they wanted to recover land in Cambodia and Laos that they had lost to the French over the years. In March of 1941, France agreed to a Thai proposal that gave the Japanese the power to arbitrate and settle the dispute.

As of July, 1941, Japan had total control of Vietnam. They stationed troops wherever they wanted and could use army and naval bases for their own military purposes. The Japanese even installed their own police force. As a result of all that had taken place, France and Japan settled down to an uneasy joint control of the area.

For the Vietnamese Nationalists this joint control was an economic nightmare. The country's wealth, long abused and exploited by the French, was now bled dry by the Japanese in order to finance their imperial military effort. Politically, the French and the Japanese began to compete for the affection of the Vietnamese.

The French had one advantage: through propaganda, they reminded the Vietnamese of their own history, especially their long struggle against domination by their Asian neighbors. The youth were then given an extensive paramilitary education, including training in the use of modern firearms. Unknown to them, the French were training a revolutionary army. The fact that the French presence in Vietnam was significant versus the limited presence of the Japanese in that country made it difficult for the Japanese to gain any real foothold with the people.

In 1941, the Japanese possessed no clear view of a future Indochina. Following their victory there, they had no intention of allowing the French to remain. Nor did they foresee any possibility of having Vietnam as a part of their postwar plans. Therefore, the Japanese were content to let France continue the financial burden of administering the colony. What the Japanese wanted was a propaganda policy that would eliminate western ideas and influence in Asia. The problem was that the Japanese did not want to see a total breakdown of French rule.

The weakness of France in protecting Vietnam against the Japanese had persuaded many from the middle class, including some landlords, to support an independence movement.

On May 10, 1941, the Vietnamese Communists assembled for two purposes: first, to organize all Vietnamese, whether workers, peasants, rich peasants, landlords, or native middle class, to work for the seizure of independence. And second, to develop guerrilla bases on Vietnamese soil, an area from which the Communists could spread their influence and which would also serve as a sample of liberated Vietnam. By the end of 1941, one-third of the villages had been organized.

In early 1943, a new man emerged to lead the Vietnamese forces in China: Ho Chi Minh.

When the Chinese supported the Vietnamese in their struggle against Japan in 1943, they received the support of the US mission in China, which virtually bankrolled the entire Chinese war effort. US policy makers had been concerned about postwar plans for Indochina because the United States depended upon Indochina for fifty-percent of its raw rubber. Japanese control of the area deprived the US of its major source of this resource. The US, in concert with Britain and Holland, cut off Japan's oil supplies. In negotiations that took place in the fall of 1941 with Japan, the United States made several demands, including the evacuation of Vietnam by Japanese forces. The Japanese response to the American proposals was the attack on Pearl Harbor.

On March 9, 1945, Japan ended nearly one-hundred years of French rule in Indochina. Shortly before midnight on that day, Japanese soldiers entered the governor general's palace and secured all the major administrative buildings, public utilities, and radio stations for the Japanese. French troops throughout the country were caught off guard. Whole regiments surrendered without a shot, though many others fought bravely even when encircled and outnumbered. Thousands of French were taken prisoner. A few hundred escaped to the mountains. There they were surprised to find a well-coordinated network of guerrillas, experienced in helping Allied soldiers, especially downed pilots, escape from the Japanese. The Vietnamese cared for many Frenchmen, helping them escape into China.

In August, 1945, a revolution took place. The Vietnamese had consistently fought Japanese aggression and fought it more effectively than the French themselves. It was only a matter of time along with a constant desire to be free that eventually won independence for Vietnam. The French were gone, the Japanese had surrendered and in Vietnam, a country deemed incapable of self-government, order prevailed. It had simply done what generations of Vietnamese had wanted to do, proclaim Vietnam's independence.

The author of Vietnam's Declaration of Independence was Ho Chi Minh. After eighty years of French rule, Vietnam was again independent and again united. However, this peace in Vietnam was to be short-lived. Already the French were regrouping. The revolution of August, 1945, was to usher in not a new era of peace for the

Vietnamese but the bloodiest and most destructive thirty years in its history.

In 1954, the United States contributed one-billion dollars to the French colonial cause in Indochina, thereby underwriting eighty percent of the French war against Vietnam. The French army, which had regained some control of the country, was defeated in Dien Beh Phu. Vietnam was again split into two states. The division was at the 17th parallel and confined the Nationalist and Communist government of Ho Chi Minh to the north. This was part of an agreement called the Geneva Accord and was signed by all involved parties. It gave Laos and Cambodia independence. Neither the North nor the South was permitted to enter into a military alliance or permit the location of bases of foreign power. Finally, the Accord stated that national elections were to be held in 1956 after which the country was to be reunited.

In 1955, South Vietnamese premier Ngo Dinh Diem took control of Saigon and caused a Communist insurrection. The established plans went up in smoke. The United States sent military counselors to help Saigon and troops to South Vietnam.

In December of 1961, President John Kennedy sent a letter to Vietnam's President Diem. In it he stated: "I have received your recent letter in which you described so cogently the dangerous condition caused by North Vietnam's efforts to take over your country. The situation in your embattled country is well known to me and to the American people. We have been deeply disturbed by the assault on your country. Our indignation has mounted as the deliberate savagery of the Communist program of assassination, kidnapping, and wanton violence became clear. Your letter underlines what our own information has convincingly shown – that the campaign of force and terror now being waged against your people and your government is supported and directed from the outside by the authorities at Hanoi. They have thus violated the provisions of the Geneva Accords designed to ensure peace in Vietnam and to which they have bound themselves in 1954. At that time, the United States, although not a party to the Accords, declared that it would view any renewal of the aggression in violation of the Agreements with grave concern and as seriously threatening international peace and security. We continue to maintain that view. In accordance with that declaration, and in response to your request, we are prepared to help the Republic of Vietnam to protect its people and to preserve its independence. We shall promptly increase our assistance to your defense effort as well as help relieve the destruction of the floods, which you describe. I have already given the orders to get those programs underway. The United States, like the Republic of Vietnam, remains devoted to the cause of peace and our primary purpose is to help your people maintain their independence. If the Communist authorities in North Vietnam will stop their campaign to destroy the Republic of Vietnam, the measures we are taking to assist your defense efforts will no longer be necessary. We shall seek to persuade the Communists to give up their attempts of force and subversion. In any case, we are confident that the Vietnamese people will preserve their independence and gain the peace and prosperity for which they have fought so hard and so long."

That same year, Kennedy stated, "Mankind must put an end to war or war will put an end to mankind."

In November of 1963, President Kennedy was assassinated and Vice-president Lyndon Johnson took the reins as President. That same year, a group of South Vietnamese officials killed Ngo Dirh Diem.

Although Vietnam was a country some 9000 miles distant from the United States, America felt that its national interest was threatened enough to fight a war there. This was due to the spread of Communism that was taking place throughout Asia. The establishment of the Iron Curtain in Europe after the Second World War, the Communist takeover of China, the Korean War and the Communist victory over the French in Vietnam all led Americans to believe that the Communists were looking to take over the entire world and, therefore, they must be stopped. Many people were afraid of the domino theory that if one Asian country fell to the Communists the others would quickly follow. The US government believed that by helping the South Vietnamese government resist the attacks of the Communist North they were helping to prevent the spread of Communism throughout the world.

In late 1964, President Johnson announced that US destroyers had been attacked without provocation by the North Vietnamese. This began the war with Vietnam. Three days later, after the passage of a resolution to assist South Vietnam, American troops were being called up for involvement in combat.

That year, Johnson said, "We still seek no wider war and we are not about to send American boys nine or ten-thousand miles away from home to do what Asian boys ought to be doing themselves."

In 1965, the US started the bombing of the supply routes in North Vietnam. These bombings continued into 1973, which was the last year American troops fought in the jungles of Vietnam.

In 1968, the North Vietnamese started huge attacks in the larger cities of South Vietnam.

The American culture has changed since the days of the Puritans and even more so since the period of World War II. The change in the conventions of language usage has been swift, in particular the common acceptance of expletives in everyday conversation. In the course of two decades, from 1950 through 1970, a shift in attitudes has marked spectacular instances of public profanity. War is the greatest trigger when it comes to a change in vocabulary. The war in Vietnam was a catalyst in the social division provoking violent protests such as the tactics used by radical students at the University of California at Berkeley from which many copycat protests emanated.

Most of the swear words used today originated in England centuries ago. What is truly interesting is that the Native American, Japanese, Malaysian and Polynesian people do not swear.

Since the 1980's there has been a shift in taboos that include a change from servile to racial terms. Black humor and a corresponding humor that makes fun of blacks as well as other ethnic races has become popular. One man's vulgarity is another man's lyric. Sensitivity by some people has in a few instances become ludicrous, i.e. the use by a white politician of the word niggardly, meaning impoverished, was taken by some blacks as being derogative toward their race because of ignorance of the word's true definition.

The shift in the twenty-first century seems to be in the area of political taboos, with all other former taboos now accepted as funny. How America has changed since the 1950's. The VietnamWar brought the changes out in full force and with those changes a significant relaxation in moral behavior. America is changing again, but the question now becomes, in what direction?

America has changed since the Vietnam War and has become carelessly free with the language from the President down, and with no respect for authority. A perfect example can be seen in the words of President Johnson back in 1972 when he was quoted as saying, "I don't want loyalty…I want *loyalty*. I want him (unknown to whom he was speaking at the time) to kiss my ass in Macy's window at high noon and to tell me it smells like roses. I want his pecker in my pocket." Johnson, in another issue that year made the comment in speaking about another subject, "It's better to have him inside the tent pissing out, than outside pissing in." Finally, in 1975, Johnson said about President Gerald Ford, "He's so dumb he can't fart and chew gum at the same time."

"The Devil tempts men through their ambition, their cupidity, or their appetite, until he comes to the profane swearer, whom he catches without any bait or reward." Horace Mann

CHAPTER EIGHT –?

"'Cheshire-Puss,' she began, 'would you tell me, please, which way I ought to go from here?' 'That depends a good deal on where you want to get to,' said the Cat. 'I don't much care where –' said Alice. 'Then it doesn't matter which way you go,' said the Cat. '—so long as I get somewhere,' Alice added as an explanation. 'Oh, you're sure to do that,' said the Cat, 'if you only walk long enough.' Alice felt that this could not be denied, so she tried another question. 'What sort of people live about here?' 'In that direction,' the Cat said, waving its right paw around, 'lives a Hatter; and in that direction,' waving the other paw, 'lives a March Hare. Visit either you like: they're both mad.' 'But I don't want to go among mad people,' Alice remarked. 'Oh, you can't help that,' said the Cat: 'we're all mad here. I'm mad. You're mad.' 'How do you know I'm mad?' said Alice. 'You must be,' said the Cat, 'or you wouldn't have come here.'"[1]

We live in a world that is utterly mad! It is no great feat to look through a kaleidoscope and see the jumble of mismatched pieces of colored glass that can represent the mismatched ideas and desires of the leaders of this world. It is only when the glass shards are put between the lenses of the kaleidoscope that they seem to hold some kind of order. But that is all an illusion; an imitation of what the real world is truly like. It is simply a reflection of the glossed-over negatives created by the governments that want to conceal their true motives to the rest of the world. The problem is that the rest of the world is no different.

Too many times is this world treated to war and death by those who are sick in their worship of vice, their love of lies, their hate of truth and their scorn for virtue. They claim to seek peace while burying their head in the sand as an ostrich or by offering bribes to those whose lot in life is to commit evil.

Here once again, can be found lunatics competing for the control of the world and the future of all humanity. Mad players in the game of power, hate-crazed and swollen with bloated ambition, lord it over opponents who give away all that they have because they are fear-crazed and would rather flee from life than hold their ground.

THE WORLD'S DISEASE

The reader who has come this far in the book will doubtless be weary and puzzled. The story of grief and pain is tiresome and baffling. How the world has fared up to this point in time within this latest age of frustration shows how sick indeed its leaders and supporters are. There are many who worship vice and lies and hate the truth and would rather favor war and death. Sick also are those who seek peace by hiding their heads or by bribing evil-doers. Yet, in the middle of the twentieth century such behavior is all but universal. Mad players of the game of power, with their insatiable ambitions, play chess on the squares of the world against opponents who play "give away" because of fear and an urge to flee from life.

What do such sufferers, apparently so different, have in common? Each is attempting to escape from the torture of worry. Each fears and, therefore, hates the world. Going outside of one's private world and into the public world, what is seen is a populace that believes they are sane. I am not really a pessimist but at times I feel that I am living in a mad house.

In America there are the isolationists, in Britain are the appeasers, in France are the submissionists, all of whom are the disciples of escape; the ones who seek safety through withdrawal from danger. What is interesting is that most people receive the kind of leadership they deserve, even if it is not what they desire.

At one point in time, Harry Truman said, "Wherever you have an efficient government, you have a dictatorship."

From the depths of an unstable middle-class have come the new elite of our time and many of the leaders of new causes are really introducing only old causes under a new regime. Look at the Mussolini's, the Hitler's, the Lenin's, the Roosevelt's, the Blum's, the Chamberlain's, the Atlee's, the Willkie's, the Lindbergh's, and the deGaulle's. All see the world through different eyes and often are utterly at odds with one another. Yet, there is a likeness in their individual and various ways when one considers these world-wide worriers and the class from which they have emanated.

Why all these worries? Because, say many of the victims, there is a "lack of confidence," too much "public extravagance," too many "unbalanced budgets," an overabundance of "governmental meddling," and so on. However, these are not causes, but the results of the economic malaise that has settled upon our world. The actual cause, found at the base, is the tyranny of time and the difficulty of spanning the chasm between yesterday and tomorrow. Men and women, the producers and consumers, are living – or trying to live – amid the streamlined gadgets of an ultra-modern industrial civilization created by the machine and spanning all the planet. The machine has long since made of all the world one market, one workshop, one playground, and one neighborhood, whose people are everywhere dependent upon one another for their livelihood and security.

The result of all this is clearly not a curse but a boon for the human race. The seeds of tragedy lay with people who did not awaken fully to the new world created by their handiwork. The practices of people in earning a living knit the world together. But the practices of the same people in preaching patriotism have torn the world apart into an ever larger number of political entities, waging tariff wars and currency wars and diplomatic wars and military wars, one against the other. Armed violence among nations is not at all the inevitable product of human nature. However, it is assuredly the inevitable product of the division of coercive authority among rival sovereignties.

Diplomacy, properly understood, is but war carried on by peaceful means – that is to say by trickery and bargaining, supported by threats of force. War is but diplomacy conducted by the open use of arms. When people live abundantly and precariously in a world society, then power politics becomes a formula for universal ruin. In the name of defense, each power strives for self-sufficiency and, thereby, hampers trade.

Martin Olson

Western mankind has the choice of reshaping its old design for politics to fit its new design for living, or of abandoning its modern design for living in order to continue playing the ancient game of power. If mankind would preserve its twentieth century world society so that it might enjoy the fruits that it has brought, it must likewise renounce the politics of power.

The prerequisites of world order are not mysterious. The experience of the human race supply the answers. Unity requires that people be bound together by a common faith in a common destiny. If they truly want peace, with the removal of the causes of worry and fear, the disparity of the present time of trouble will pass away. Those who live in the past can never prevail against those who have met the challenge of the future. Those who are utterly lacking in imagination and ideas cannot conquer those gifted with both. The task of the American leaders is to inspire their peoples with a positive purpose worthy of sacrifice and devotion. Their task is further to inspire the vanquished with a vision of hope in a free world order, for without the aid of the vanquished the continent can never be re-won.

Power politics is approaching its twilight. Man still has a will to live. He will choose the way, which offers the hope for life.

The change that looms ahead is a change from an age of violence and warring states to a time of peace for all mankind. Embattled people will win the mastery of tomorrow if they will but undertake this task. If they will not, they will fail and fall and yield the future to the hosts of the Caesars. The task of union is reserved for

154

those who see its need and who act courageously to bring the gift of ordered peace to humanity. Let those who are worthy take charge.

As we face yet another *opportunity* for war, based upon the actions currently being taken by our government, one must stop and look back over history and make a decision as to whether or not this is our best course. How can any country afford another holocaust? Would it not make more sense to try for a reshaping of the old way of doing things including its design for politics so that we might enjoy a new design for living? Or, do we continue on playing the old game, which is founded on the politics of power?

Most people would quickly say that they would want to opt for the first choice of reshaping rather than play the power game. However, in order to do that, one must realize that such a step is not easily taken. It does not simply happen because one makes a firm resolution to avoid entanglement and mind one's own business. The end result of such an action will quickly make victims of those who believe the *laissez-faire* attitude works.

Of course, neither can it be done by breaking up nations and empires into smaller and weaker units. It can only be done by replacing anarchy in government because that is incompatible with unity and order in world business and world civilization. Anarchy yields poverty and grief as has been seen most recently in the battle in Iraq. The country's leader, Saddam Hussein, in his exercise of power, took control of all the money belonging to the people, leaving them penniless. This, in turn, fostered a growth of bitterness and anxiety and acts of viciousness and cruelty among the populace. The cure for anarchy is order. And the price of order is government with power sufficient to impose peace and protect justice by a force, which cannot be challenged. Unfortunately, sometimes the only way to reach that point is by employing the vestiges of war. The task of the leaders is to inspire their people with a positive purpose worthy of sacrifice and devotion.

At the outbreak of the Korean War, President Truman was persuaded to send arms to the French in Indochina in order to contain the People's Republic of China. The struggle in Indochina became less a question of self-determination to an integral part of the existing Cold War. By 1954, the US was contributing one-billion dollars to the French Colonial cause in Indochina. This translated into the underwriting of some eighty percent of the French war against the Vietnamese. Truman thought that the outcome of US intervention would give the French a chance to regain their colony; it did not. He further thought that the final victory would be democracy for China; it did not.

The conclusion to World War II meant only one thing because of the way in which the US negotiated the cease-fire. The US would occupy and rule Japan for years until the Japanese regained their strength and became a major world economic force. A divided Korea was liberated from Japan but then engaged in a civil war that drew the United States into battle against the People's Republic of China.

When the superpower struggle was over, there really had been no winner. People still suffered, starved, and died because they had not learned how to live at peace. The most frightening scientific invention to come out of the war was the ability to convert matter into energy and, thereby, create a nuclear bomb. That invention continues to develop to a mightier and more devastating device. A further effect of the Truman years would be the eventual conflict with Vietnam. With the expansion of machinery in our society, especially the mechanization of war apparatus, the need for fossil fuel also increased.

Now we are in an age when there is a reliance on the oil found in the Middle Eastern countries; this has become a necessary commodity. And in the Middle East there is a distrust of the American people. They have seen how we have handled ourselves in past situations and we, in some ways, have acted no better than they have in our means for handling conflict and politics. The politics of power reigns once more. And again we face the probability of a war. What is most disconcerting is that a battle involving the United States with the Arab nations may never lead to peace in that part of the world and the gap between war and peace may grow ever more distant.

America led the free world through the Cold War and into the hot wars of Korea, Vietnam, Kuwait, and Iraq. Still people suffered and continue to suffer, many starving and dying in conflicts because we have not learned to live in peace. The only thing that past wars have taught us is that man's worst enemy is man.

America is like a son growing up and taking over the family business as is often done in Europe. As in all families where the son inherits the business, he has forgotten or perhaps did not study the past history so he goes about making mistakes thinking that he is

157

better and smarter than his parents. Some people rebel because they know something is not right yet they do not know what it is. In some instances, they realize that there is a plot against people, one that will always exist, because government has always used people for its own ends. Government seems to be hostile toward the governed. This is not a new story; the conspirators have varied from ear to era, depending upon the political or economic situations in various countries.

During the time of Karl Marx conspiracies and conspirators became one, with one aim, objective and determination. And that conspiracy had nothing to do with ideological ideas, or materialism, or any other of the many thoughts fed to the masses. It really had nothing to do with race or religion because the conspiracy was beyond the concept of good and evil. The Caesars that were put in power found their positions because of the maneuvering of the conspirators and the nation's people in America, Japan, Britain, Russia, Europe and South America, found themselves helpless. They will remain helpless until they become aware of their real enemy.

Democracy, according to Webster's Dictionary, is a government by the people in which the supreme power is vested in the people and exercised directly by them or by their elected agents under a free electoral system. In theory it looks great, however in practice it can be seen that these agents become Caesars controlled by the elite of the conspiracy.

People are always looking for a utopia but there is none on this planet. The electors are reaching for men of destiny and prophets of order in a complex society coping with rising expectations, gigantic projects, demographic imbalance, and external threats. Order and social control will be the ultimate choice. As yet, such men of destiny and prophets of order are still nowhere to be found.

During the past 200 years, industrialization has been the greatest force for social change in history. It began with England's textile manufacturing in the 1780's and was followed by the iron and steel industry in the 19th century, which led to the combining of science and technology and an unending cycle of invention and discovery throughout the world. This can be reflected in something as uniquely modern as today's cellular telephones and the dynamic increases that particular device has seen from a modest eleven million units in 1990 to more than nine-hundred and ninety-five million units in 2001. A similar explosion can be seen with the phenomenal Internet computer hosting companies that are now the rage throughout every country on the face of the earth. That business has grown from a base of 376,000 users in 1990 to more than 147,344,723 in 2001 and continuing to climb at an even faster pace.

Some other interesting statistics to look at are that 61% of the world population live and work in Asia, with only 12% in Europe and 5% in the United States. While the US has the largest economy and the largest industrial, manufacturing, and services output in the world, with Japan as a close second, the US also has the highest deficit while Japan has the highest surplus.

The largest producer of agriculture is China, with the US coming in second. Still China needs help in feeding the 77 million person annual increase in its population. Compare that with the countries of Canada, Norway and Australia that boast the highest degree of human development and quality of life.

What do these figures mean? Not much except to show how close the nations are in their effort to survive; hopefully without any conflicts.

During the Harry Truman years as President, when the men and women of the military brought World War II to a close and ended the horrific genocide, the postwar world began with a feeling of optimism. However, students of history realized that the real war was not over; it would continue into the next millennium. Perhaps it is the ghost of President Wilson still lurking from 1919 when the Treaty of Versailles was voted down in Washington and Wilson warned that a world war would occur with a span of twenty-odd years.

My purpose in writing this book was to not only give a reflection of past history, but to arm the citizens of our country to be the most informed people as to what transpired up until this point in time. It is necessary to know the actions and inactions of the countries of this world since 1900 and to have those factors spelled out through World War I, World War II, Korea, Vietnam and Iraq.

It is now 2003 and our country is facing the problems created in Iraq, North Korea and whichever countries come next. Compounding these problems is the fact that the world itself has become so small that what affects one part, affects the whole, like it or not. The world looking on while the President of the United States,

George W. Bush, decides to go to war against Iraq. At the same time, North Korea sits by also threatening America.

The greatest problem with North Korea is that it has no assets other than nuclear bombs and a large military. Consider that against Iraq that has limited armor, some biological weapons of mass destruction and loaded with oil-based assets – a very saleable commodity that can be easily traded or sold.

In the eyes of Islam, America becomes an evil force, one that takes away the assets of Iraq as well as the rest of the Arab countries. America looks at Islam as the people who harbor terrorists. Each sees only what it wants to see. And neither one understands the other, most especially the failure of the United States to understand the Arab mind. Once again, history has not changed.

The most frightful outcome of the Islamic faith is the fact that here are poor people for the most part who are looking for something to hold on to in their meager lives. Islam gives them a place to hang their hat. So, the faith grows in numbers. One thing that the leaders of the Muslim faith stress is the fault-finding it can use to give the people something upon which to cast the reasons for their condition. America becomes the enemy. Even when the US intercedes on behalf of a troubled and victimized people, does it become the target for their wrath. If the American people do not study history to see what has happened in the past, especially with those who have wanted to appease the ones who make the most noise, they will find themselves in less than twenty years, as a consequence of the Islamic growth, being challenged by a threat like none other this world has ever seen.

The final conclusion could be a world run by Muslims and in which the previously free Americans become their pawns. What will help lead to this? The enormous sums of money being made by those Middle Eastern countries from the sale of oil.

As of 2000, Iraq had oil reserves of 100,000,000 barrels with a sustainable capacity of five million barrels a day. They have a refining capacity of 318,500 barrels of crude oil per day. Oil is the natural resource that will bring us to the brink of war once again. There is no doubt in my mind. And where there is a great potential of oil reserves in the Arabian nations, the US will have its mightiest struggle in trying to wage a war while promoting peace in an area that does not want Americans. The vicious cycle of the history of war is bound to repeat itself. I can only hope that the American people, and to a greater extent their political representatives, will pay attention to the lessons that history can teach us. If not, we are a doomed nation with little or no chance of recovery.

IRAN, KUWAIT, IRAQ

There are three countries – Iran, Kuwait, and Iraq – facing each other across the Persian Gulf. All three have a common commodity – petroleum. All three were part of the ancient Persian Empire. And all three share the same religious faith – Islam – with the same distrust of Westerners.

Islam is hard to suppress and harder to filter out of politics. It is a political faith with its name implying a way of life as well as a system of religious beliefs. Islam is intended to be a code of civil laws, which it sometimes practices. And it is for a few, a convenient method of control.

The oil boon of the 1960's and 70's provided funds for social progress. When the boon ended, economic difficulties arose. Revolution began again because such actions are easy. Reformation is hard and few have the knowledge to achieve it. One man's holy war can be another man's terrorism. The biggest problem, as that found in the entire world, is money. For Islam it is oil and money – at least for those who want to be another Caesar.

The region now called Iran was occupied by the Medes and the Persians in about 1500 BC, and up to the 1940's has had many rulers including British and Russian. On January 16, 1979, the ruling Sheikh and his family fled Iran after he imposed martial law in September of 1978. The Sheikh was a friend of the United States and had their support. After January 16, 1979, Ayotollah Khomeini, an exiled cleric, took over and established an Islamic Theocracy. He proceeded with his plan for revitalizing Islamic traditions. Militants invaded the US Embassy and took hostages as a result of the economic boycott by the United States. The hostage crisis ended 444 days later with an agreement by the United States not to interfere in Iranian affairs, the cancellation of US damage claims against Iran, the release of eight billion dollars in frozen Iranian assets, an apology and return of assets held by the former Imperial family. These conditions were met and 52 American hostages were released on January 20, 1980.

On September 20, 1980, Iraq invaded Iran and in March of 1982 Iran launched an offensive and regained land taken by Iraq. This conflict dragged on through August, 1988 when a cease fire was agreed upon. A conflict started over control of the Shatt-Al-Arab waterway between Iran and Iraq and ended at the same location. What a waste of energy. Khomeini died in June, 1989. Mohammad Khotani then became president and established greater social and political freedoms. He had many trials to overcome as he tried to maintain a middle course. His goal was to make Iran a nation of lasting pluralism with an Islamic form of democracy.

Kuwait is believed to be a part of the early civilization that existed in the third millennium BC. It obtained British protection in 1897 and had that support until it ended in 1961 when it gave Kuwait independence along with military aid on request. Oil was discovered in the 1930's and Kuwait proved to have twenty percent of the world's known oil reserves. Since 1946, it has been the world's second largest oil exporter. In July of 1990, Iraq blamed Kuwait for falling oil prices and in August of that year, invaded Kuwait and set up a pro-Iraq government. Iraq drained Kuwait of its economic resources. A coalition of Arab and Western military forces drove large troops from Kuwait in a mere four days, from February 23 to 27, ending the Persian Gulf War. The private Swiss Trust that I worked for as assistant to the Chairman, Mihaly, built and financed the Kuwait Hospital in the 1970's.

Iraq was the cradle of civilization that began as an advanced civilization by 4000 BC. The British in World War I occupied most of Mesopotamia and gave a mandate over the area in 1920. The British renamed the area Iraq and recognized it as a kingdom in 1922. In 1932, it received full independence. During World War II, Britain again occupied Iraq.

In 1968, a junta led by Major General Ahmed Hassan Ali-Bakr of the Ba'ath Party and his second in command, Saddam Hussein, took control and ended decades of political instability. It became one of the world's leading producers of oil. It used the revenue from this resource to develop one of the strongest military forces in that region. On July 16, 1979, Saddam Hussein took control of the presidency and eventually developed an international reputation for repression, human rights abuses, and terrorism. Hussein had early training as a former bravo and bouncer at political meetings. It was a good training ground for his history of abuses. He used his might almost excessively against fellow Muslims. He also claimed to be a descendant of the Shiite culture-hero, Ali.

Iraq invaded Iran in 1980 over water rights between Iraq and Iran. The war lasted eight years and cost approximately 150,000 lives. It was all for nothing as not one inch of land was gained as it ended where it started. It reflected the same mental thinking as that of North Korea.

I was instructed to go to Iraq to meet with the government in 1984 while I was on another project in the Sudan. At the last minute I was told to cancel the visit. I was in the Sudan for two weeks after

Vice-president Bush was there when I had received the call to go to Iraq.

In July of 1990, Hussein claimed that Kuwait was flooding the market with oil and forcing oil prices down. In August of that year, he attacked Kuwait and in four days he lost that conflict. The irony is that in the 1980's the United States met with Hussein and assisted Iraq in their war against Iran because the US hated Khomeini and Iran. In the 1990 conflict with Kuwait, the US joined with the United Nations and forced Iraq to leave Kuwait. Iraq lost the Gulf War. Confusion in a mad, mad world.

Now in 2003, President George W. Bush stated that Hussein had weapons of mass destruction and he needed to be removed from Iraqi leadership. Bush stated that he hated Hussein and wanted him taken out, so on March 20, the United States attacked Iraq. This was the first time in American history that the US had attacked a foreign country first, and vowed to finish the job in removing Hussein. The genie was out of the bottle and will probably never be returned. Hatred is a very powerful energy and it consumes a person as well as groups, regions and nations.

The United States gave this conflict the name Iraqi Freedom. Freedom will be won by the US and Britain but peace will still be out of sight. The genie has made sure that it will not happen during most of our lives.

As stated in earlier chapters, the Caesars whom the conspirators put in power have other plans that come into play following a war or conflict. They have a hidden agenda that is not always discernable. Looking back at the past, there is always a personal reason why a war or conflict was started and most times it was for personal financial gain or power.

There is talk of a holy war by Islam. One must understand that Islam is extremely big with 1.3 billion population, or 21 percent of the population of the planet. The total population of the world was 6,007,486,448 in August of 1999 and growing at a rate of approximately 70,000,000 per year. Islam is too big for coherent political action, and too diverse to be a single unit. To change this course, there is no surge of revivalism that could be big enough to pull all the people together. When a political action begins to roll, leaders may ride the wave but rarely succeed in taking control of its power. They have never generated political action for a long period even with a common enemy.

When I had dealings in the Sudan and in Saudi, Arabia, I discovered that one had to complete one's ideas in a short time or the attention of the Middle Eastern person one was meeting would be cut off because of the short attention span of that person. The attention span is short, but long on memory. The big problem for the West is the *small* groups that may cause problems.

After Iraq, there is North Korea once again. With their one-million member army and nuclear bomb ability, they are sure to be a test for both the United Nations and the United States. President Bush had stated that he hated the ruler of North Korea. We can see the genie at work again. Let everyone pray that wisdom prevails.

"It is truly a mad-mad world 'war' – that mad-mad game the world so loves to play." Sw:ft

In the children's book, *Gulliver's Travels*, in the last chapter, the captain was abandoned on an island to fend for himself. The island was controlled by horses. They asked the captain to tell them about himself.

He stated, "I am an Englishman where horses pull carriages and ploughs. We use war to settle arguments and make guns and bullets to do our killing. The rich have all the money and the poor have none. We have many criminals and…"

"Stop!" the horse said. "You are no different than the others that live on the island. If I throw enough food for fifty into a room, the stronger one will take it all and leave none for the others."

The horse explained that they live together in peace and were very honest, have no evil thoughts, are governed by reason, and their main rules are friendship and kindness.

It is too bad that this is a children's fantasy and about animals and not humans.

* * * * *

There are three classes of people in the world. The first learn from their own experience – these are the wise. The second learn from the experience of others – these are the happy. The third neither learn from their own experience nor the experience of others – these are the fools. Remember Hell is God's justice, heaven is his love, earth is his long suffering.

Every tomorrow has two handles. We can take hold of it with the handle of anxiety or the handle of faith.

Real freedom comes from the mastery through knowledge of historic conditions and race character, which makes possible a free and intelligent use of experience for the purpose of progress.

Hamilton Wright Mabie

AFTERWORD

Some readers of my first book, *Iron Shoes,* have asked why did I work for the Swiss Trust Chairman without receiving pay? The average American cannot understand doing something for nothing, as it would appear, and then they add that they would never work for anyone without receiving money. If there was no monetary benefit, they would leave, quit. It is not in the American culture to do otherwise.

Well, to answer this question that may be seen as a flaw in my composition, I have to explain my behavior. Once I decide that the goals and mission of a person such as the Chairman of the Swiss Trust are worthy and I make a commitment, I will not leave my obligation. Having started a project, I must do everything possible to complete the task. To some people this may be a flaw in my personal framework.

When I was sent to Kartoum in the Sudan, and observed the people and their inability to restart projects such as their abandoned textile mills, which were a result of a lack of funding, and once I had the taste of Africa in my system, I was hooked. I had to do everything I could to help. I stayed with the Chairman of the Swiss Trust, not only to be re-tooled by him in my thinking and not think like an American, but to try to persuade him to allow me to help lesser countries like the Sudan, Sierra Leone and others in Africa. I did not win because his goal was medical research and the building of a medical research center on an internationally global scale.

After caring from my wife over the two years she was dying from cancer, my objective to help Africa was over. I struggled along with my wife in her suffering and only by the Grace of God was I kept alive and did I manage to pay for all of her medical bills. Somehow I survived this long ordeal. I do not regret going to Africa and staying with the Chairman of the Swiss Trust. If I had known the Doctor and had been re-tooled by him before I built the Samoset Hotel, I never would have lost the resort by the takeover of the mortgage company after I had built it. It was not to be so one goes on to the next task.

I am at a point now where I could not care less about what people think, especially those who would question my working for no money. I have discovered that I do not have to answer to anyone save God, my wife, and myself. I make my own decisions and choose to take whichever road presents itself and appeals to me.

A FINAL NOTE

As I began this book with an Alice in Wonderland theme, I wanted to end this journey with Alice in Wonderland.

"Alice and the caterpillar stared at each other for some time in silence. At last the caterpillar took the pipe out of its mouth and addressed her in a lazy, sleepy voice: 'Who are you?' the odd-looking creature asked. This was not an encouraging conversation opener, but Alice replied, 'I – I hardly know, Sir. I know who I was when I got up this morning, but I must have changed several times since then.' 'What do you mean by that?' the caterpillar asked sternly. 'Explain yourself at once.' 'I can't explain myself,' Alice replied, 'because I'm not myself, you see.' 'I don't see,' said the caterpillar. 'I'm afraid I can't put it more clearly,' Alice went on, 'for I can't understand myself, being so many different sizes in one day is very confusing.' 'It is not,' said the caterpillar. 'Well, perhaps you haven't found it so yet,' Alice snapped back, 'but one day you will turn into a butterfly and then you'll feel odd, won't you?' 'Not a bit,' the caterpillar answered. 'Well, perhaps your feelings are different,' said Alice. 'All I know is it would feel very odd to me.' 'You,' said the caterpillar angrily, 'Who are you?' This brought them back to the very beginning. Alice was getting fed up with the insect's remarks, so she said, 'I think you ought to tell me who you are first.' 'Why?' the caterpillar asked. Alice did not know quite how to answer that. As she did not have a good reply, she gave up and began to walk away.

'Wait!' said the caterpillar. 'Come back. I have something important to say.' Alice turned around and listened. 'Keep your temper,' it said. 'Is that all?' said Alice annoyed. 'No,' said the caterpillar. It paused a few moments before continuing. 'So you think you're changed, do you?' 'I'm afraid I am sick,' Alice said. 'I can't remember things as I used to, and I don't stay the same size for more than ten minutes at a time.' 'What size do you want to be?' 'Oh, I'm not particular,' Alice said. 'I just don't like changing so often, you see.' 'I don't see' the caterpillar said rudely. 'Are you content now?' 'Well, I would like to be a little larger, sir, if you wouldn't mind,' Alice replied. 'Three inches is a terrible height to be.' [1]

Martin Olson

Great Events of the Twentieth Century

Years Between Conflicts	Year	Conflict	Major Event
	1904-5	Russo-Japanese War	1901 – Trans-Siberian Railway
			1903 – Suffragette Movement
9	1914	World War I	
3	1917	Russian Revolution	1919 – Atom split
			1922 – Insulin discovered
			1926 – Television invented
9	1928	Wall Street Crash	1928 – Penicillin discovered
5	1933	Hitler become Chancellor	1930 – Gas turbine invented
		of Germany	
3	1936-9	Spanish Civil War	1935 – Radar invented
1	1939	Germany invades Poland	
3	1942	World War II	1942 – Computers invented
3	1945	Atomic Bomb used in war	1946 – 1st Meeting of the UN
3	1948-9	Israeli War for Independence	1948 – Ghandi assassinated
1	1950	Korean War	1949 – NATO formed
2	1952	Hydrogen Bomb tested	1954 – Russia has 1st Nuclear
			Power Station
3	1956	Egypt seizes Suez Canal	
		Hungarian uprising	
4	1962	US Troops move into South	
		Vietnam	
		Cuban missile crisis	1963 – President Kennedy
			Assassinated
3	1965	Cultural Revolution – China	
2	1967	Arab-Israeli War	1968 – Martin Luther King
			Assassinated
2	1969	Czechoslovakia suppressed	
		Russia	
4	1973	Arab-Israeli War	1973 – US Troops leave Vietnam
5	1978	Iran-Iraq War	1974 – President Nixon resigns
1	1979	US Hostage rescue in Iran fails	
3	1982	Israel invades Lebanon	1981 – Anwar Sadat Assassinated
6	1988	Iran-Iraq War ends	1986 – Challenger Rocket disaster
1	1989	Eastern Block Revolution	1987 – Stock Market Crash
			1989 – Student protest in China
1	1990	Iraq invades Kuwait	
1	1991	Gulf War in Iraq	1991 – USSR breaks up
1		Civil War in Yugoslavia	
1	1992	US intervenes in Somalia	1992 – Muslim rule in Afghanistan
			Yugoslavia breaks up
1	1994	Civil War in Rwanda	1993 – Israel allows PLO self-rule
		Cease Fire in Ireland	
5	1995-2000	Iraqi War / UN intervention	
		Israel – Palestine Conflict	
1	2001	Iraq / UN / Israel / Palestine	2001 – 9/11 World Trade Center
			Disaster
1	2002	Iraq / UN / Israel / Palestine	
1	2003	Iraqi War / North Korea threat	2003 – Columbia Rocket disaster
		to US	

The following pages depict some of the projects I have been involved in over the years with governmental agencies in the United States and with the Swiss Trust.

The first photograph is of the Samoset Resort in Rockport, Maine. After I purchased this property, the finance people I had been working with saw the potential for this vacation and conference facility and squeezed me out of ownership.

The second photograph is at a meeting I had with the Archbishop of Cyprus in Greece. My purpose, as explained to me by the Miami Group for whom I worked, was to arrange contracts for a building project on the island. My real purpose, as I discovered at a later time, was to obtain information about the military on the island for an agency known as "The Company." To this day I believe it was for the CIA or the NSA.

The third set of documents outlined my work as assistant to the Swiss Trust and its Chairman, Dr. Sandor Mihaly. It shows one of his corporations, Complex Industries Holdings, and the transfer of enormous sums of money for projects to be jointly ventured with Japan. I was also the courier who carried these sums into the United States.

The fourth set of documents refer to the MacArthur Funds-Japanese reparation moneys that were given to Japan after World War II in exchange for redemption notes, which today would be worth over a trillion dollars, but were made to disappear by Richard Nixon during his bid for the presidency.

The fifth set of instruments pertain to one of the Swiss Trust's other projects called the Silent Development Program. This was Dr. Mihaly's medical research center to be built with the use of some of the funds in the Trust. The site for the project was Palm Beach, Florida.

The sixth outline is for a number of projects the Swiss Trust anticipated to establish in Asia over the years.

The seventh item is a flow chart of the Swiss Trust.

The final item is the last letter sent to me by Dr. Mihaly in which the medical project was now at a point to begin construction.

As the commentators on the Fox News Channel say, "We report, you decide." This is a mad, mad world. The caesars are increasingly active throughout the world.

"If men could learn from history, what lessons it might teach us! But passion and party blind our eyes, and the light which experience gives is a lantern on the stern, which shines only on the waves behind us."

Coleridge

New Samoset

Archbishop – Cyprus

LAW OFFICES

NISHIMURA & SANADA

TOSHIRO NISHIMURA
IUKIHIKO SANADA
MOTOHIKO AIBA
KATSURO TANAKA
MASAHIRO SHIMOJO
AKIRA KOSUGI
EIZO MATSUO
MASARU ONO
EIICHI KASHIKURA
EMIKO KASAHARA
KOICHI KUSANO
TOMOHIRO TOHYAMA
TAKASHI YONEDA
SATOSHI OGISHI
HITOMI OSHIKIRI
HIDEAKI OZAWA
AKIMITSU KAMORI
KATSU SENGOKU
RYOSUKE ITO
TAKANOBU TAKEHARA
KEN KAWABATA
SACHIO WATANABE

MASAHITO AMANO
AKITOSHI NAKAMURA
SHINICHI TAKAHASHI
ATSUO DOHKE
HIROYUKI SHIMIZU
ATSUSHI NAITO
HIROYUKI TEZUKA
MASAHIRO UENO
MITSUKO MIYAGAWA
MASAKAZU IWAKURA
HIROTO TERASHIMA
SHINTO TERAMOTO
OSAMU ISHIHARA
KOZO KAWAI
MITSUHIRO KAMIYA
TOSHIHIRO MAEDA
YOSHIKO OSHIMA

HIDETOSHI ASAKURA *
TSUNEMASA TERAI *
* CURRENTLY ON LEAVE

4TH FLOOR
KASUMIGASEKI BUILDING
2-5, KASUMIGASEKI 3-CHOME
CHIYODA-KU, TOKYO 100
JAPAN

OF COUNSEL
MASATOMI KOMATSU
TAKAHISA SUGANO

TELEPHONE: (03) 593-3 9 I I
TELEX: J 27691 JURISTS
CABLE: JURISTS TOKYO
TELECOPIER: (03) 508-6289
          (03) 591-4537
          (03) 593-3916
          (03) 593-3909

April 25, 1989

Dr. ▓▓▓▓▓▓▓▓▓▓
Chairman
▓▓▓▓▓▓▓▓▓▓▓▓▓▓▓▓▓▓▓▓▓▓▓▓.

Dear Dr. ▓▓▓▓▓:

This is to report to you the actions we have taken pursuant to your request.

First, we called on April 24, 1989 Ms. Uchida of U.S. Embassy in Tokyo at 03-224-5645, and obtained from her the following telephone numbers at the U.S. State Department:

      202-634-4000
      202-647-2912   Secretary to Mr. William Breer

      202-647-2913   Direct number to Mr. William Breer,
                     Director, Office of Japanese
                     Affairs, East Asia and Pacific
                     Affairs.

Then, we called Mr. William Breer at 202-647-2912 at 10:00 p.m. April 24, 1989 (Tokyo time), and he confirmed with us the following points:

1.   At the request of Mr. Olson of Complex Industries
     Holdings Ltd. ("CIH"), Mr. Breer was expecting our
     call.

2.   Mr. Breer had a meeting with Mr. Olson and he
     believes he has received from Mr. Olson the
     following letters:

179

A. **Letter, dated January 23, 1989**

    addressed to the:

    Secretary of Treasury, Nicholas P. Brady

    signed by Mr. Martin Olson, on behalf of
    Dr. ████████ Chairman, outlining the entire
    program concerning the joint ventures with
    Japanese companies, the effect concerning the
    trade deficit in conjunction with Japan and
    the effect to the U.S. budget deficit.

B. **Letter, dated January 24, 1989, No. 92315/424**

    addressed to:

    Secretary Brady, signed by Dr. Mihaly

    confirming the explanation made by Mr. Olson,
    outlining the international political global
    effect of CIH's project.

C. **Letter, dated January 25, 1989**

    addressed to:

    Treasury Department, to Meg Lundsager

    containing various legal aspects, inside of
    U.S.A.

D. **Letter, dated February 1, 1989**

    addressed to:

    **Department of Commerce, Secretary of
    Commerce, Robert Mosbacher**

    outlining the trade relating mechanism.

E. **Letter, dated February 1, 1989**

    addressed to:

    Chief of Staff Governor Sununu

    thanking him for all of his arrangements.

We trust the foregoing is responsive to your request. If you need any further assistance, please call.

Very truly yours,

for Masahiro Shimojo

Martin Olson

Complex Industries Holdings Ltd.

会長　Sandor Mihaly 殿

親愛なる ~~██████~~ 殿

　この手紙は、貴殿の依頼で我々が行ったことの内容を貴殿に伝えるものです。

　第1に、我々は、1989年4月24日、03-224-5645番に電話し、東京にある米国大使館の内田女史と話し、彼女から米国国務省の以下の電話番号を教えられました。

```
202-634-4000
202-647-2912    William Breer 氏の秘書
202 647 2913    East Asia and Pacific Affairs 及 Japanese
                Affairs 課の課長 William Breer 氏の直通番号
```

　次に我々は、1989年4月24日午後10時(東京時間)に202-647-2912番に電話し、William Breer 氏と話しました。そこで彼は、我々に対し以下のことを確認しました。

1　~~Complex Industries Holdings~~ Ltd. (「CIH」)の Olson 氏の依頼で Breer 氏は、我々の電話を待っていた。

2　Breer 氏は Olson 氏と会談したことがあり、Olson 氏から以下の手紙を受取ったと思う。

　(イ)　<u>1989年1月23日付の手紙</u>
　　　　で
　　　　<u>財務省長官 Nicholas P. Brady</u>
　　　　宛の ~~██████~~ 氏の代理人 Martin Olson 氏により署名されたもの。これには日本企業との合弁事業に関する全計画、日本との貿易不均衡及び米国の財政赤字に対する影響の概要が記載されていた。

　(ロ)　<u>1989年1月24日付手紙(92315/424)</u>
　　　　で
　　　　<u>Mihaly 氏が署名し Brady 長官</u>
　　　　に宛たもの。これは、Olson 氏の説明を確認するもので、またCIHの計画が国際政治に与える影響の概要が記されていた。

(ハ)　1989年1月25日付の手紙

　　　　　で

財務省の Meg Lundsager

宛のもの。これには米国内での各種法的側面についての記載があった。

(二)　1989年2月1日付の手紙

　　　　　で

商務省長官 Robert Mosbacher

宛のもの。これには通商関連のメカニズムについて記載されていた。

(ホ)　1989年2月1日付手紙

　　　　　で

Cheif of Staff Governor である Sununu

宛のもの。これは彼が行った手配について謝意を述べるものであった。

　我々は、以上が貴殿の依頼を満たすものと信じています。更に何かお手伝いすることがあればお電話下さい。

　　　　　　　　　　　　　　　　　　　　　　　　敬　具

　　　　　　　　　　　　　　　　　　　弁護士　下　條　正　浩

以上正訳しました。

弁護士　高　橋　真

183

G E N E R A L   R E P O R T

LATEST IMPORTS

Number   890427

April 27, 1989
Page one

Latest imports of ~~Complex Industries Holdings Ltd.~~

"E1"   Report number 33-CNA 890429-A. Yen denominated financial
            instruments of approximately five billion USD to be brought
(Import)   back into the USA on April 29, 1989 BECAUSE JAPANESE
            POLITICAL TURMOIL REQUIRES DELAY IN PROCESSING. Report filed
            with US Commissioner of Customs Washington D.C. on April 28,
            1989 by Certified mail P 060 111 526.

"E2"   Report number 33-CN 890429-B. Yen denominated financial
            instruments of approximately one billion five hundred sixty
(Import)   five million USD returned to USA on April 29, 1989 BECAUSE
            JAPANESE POLITICAL TURMOIL REQUIRES DELAY IN PROCESSING.
            Reported to US Commissioner of Customs Washington D.C. by
            Certified mail P 060 111 526 on April 28, 1989.

"E3"   Report number 33-CNC 890429-C. Yen denominated financial
            instruments of approximately five billion USD brought to USA
(Import)   on April 29, 1989 BECAUSE JAPANESE POLITICAL TURMOIL REQUIRES
            DELAY IN PROCESSING. Reported to US Commissioner of Customs
            Washington D.C. by Certified mail P 060 111 526 on April 28,
            1989. FIRST ENTRY INTO USA UNDER THE DIRECTION OF COMPLEX
            INDUSTRIES HOLDINGS LTD.

S U M M A R Y

```
Estimated USD amount Report number 33-CNA 890429 A  = $ 5,000,000,000.-- **
Estimated USD amount Report number 33-CN  890429 B  = $ 1,565,000,000.-- **
Estimated USD amount Report number 33-CNC 890429 C  = $ 5,000,000,000.-- **
Estimated total USD amount for all three Reports    = $11,565,000,000.-- **
Estimated USD amount for earned interest **         = $ 4,435,000,000.-- **
Estimated USD total amount for Principal & Interest = $16,000,000,000.-- **
```

**These estimated amounts are depending on the present exchange rate of the
  yen and the U.S. dollar.

MAY 0 1 1989

President

184

Customs Use Only		DEPARTMENT OF THE TREASURY UNITED STATES CUSTOMS SERVICE	OMB No. 1515-0079
		REPORT OF INTERNATIONAL	This form is to be filed with the United States Customs Service
Control No.		**TRANSPORTATION OF CURRENCY**	Privacy Act Notification
31 USC 5316; 31 CFR 103.23 and 103.25		**OR MONETARY INSTRUMENTS**	on reverse
Please Type or Print			

PART I - FOR INDIVIDUAL DEPARTING FROM OR ENTERING THE UNITED STATES

1. NAME (Last or family, first and middle)	2. IDENTIFYING NO. (See instructions)	3. DATE OF BIRTH (Mo./Day/Yr.)
~~[redacted]~~		02 ⎸ 05 ⎸ 28

4. PERMANENT ADDRESS IN UNITED STATES OR ABROAD	5. OF WHAT COUNTRY ARE YOU A CITIZEN/SUBJECT?
P.O. Box 15580 Newport Beach, California 92658	USA

6. ADDRESS WHILE IN THE UNITED STATES	7. PASSPORT NO. & COUNTRY
same as above	(USA)

8. U.S. VISA DATE	9. PLACE UNITED STATES VISA WAS ISSUED	10. IMMIGRATION ALIEN NO. (if any)

11. CURRENCY OR MONETARY INSTRUMENT WAS: (Complete 11A or 11B)

A. EXPORTED		B. IMPORTED	
Departed From: (City in U.S.)	Arrived At: (Foreign City/Country)	From: (Foreign City/Country)	At: (City in U.S.)
		Tokyo, Japan	Los Angeles, Ca

PART II - FOR PERSON SHIPPING MAILING OR RECEIVING CURRENCY OR MONETARY INSTRUMENTS

12. NAME (Last or family, first and middle)	13. IDENTIFYING NO. (See instructions)	14. DATE OF BIRTH (Mo./Da./Yr.)
~~COMPLEX INDUSTRIES HOLDINGS, Ltd~~	~~[redacted]~~	

15. PERMANENT ADDRESS IN UNITED STATES OR ABROAD	16. OF WHAT COUNTRY ARE YOU A CITIZEN/SUBJECT?
725 Market Street Wilmington, Delaware	

17. ADDRESS WHILE IN THE UNITED STATES	18. PASSPORT NO. & COUNTRY
P.O. Box 15580 Newport Beach, California 92659	

19. U.S. VISA DATE	20. PLACE UNITED STATES VISA WAS ISSUED	21. IMMIGRATION ALIEN NO. (if any)

22. CURRENCY OR MONETARY INSTRUMENTS	23. CURRENCY OR MONETARY INSTRUMENTS	NAME AND ADDRESS	24. IF THE CURRENCY OR MONETARY INSTRUMENT WAS MAILED, SHIPPED, OR TRANSPORTED COMPLETE BLOCKS A AND B.
DATE SHIPPED Apr. ,89	☐ Shipped To	Complex Industries Holdings Ltd see (15) (17) above JAPANESE POLITICAL TURMOIL	A. Method of Shipment (Auto, U.S. Mail, Public Carrier, etc.) Courier of ~~[redacted]~~
DATE RECEIVED Apr. 29,89	[X] Received From	REQUIRES DELAY IN PROCESSING (see attach report nbr. 890427)	B. Name of Transporter/Carrier (1) above on Japan Air #62

PART III - CURRENCY AND MONETARY INSTRUMENT INFORMATION (SEE INSTRUCTIONS ON REVERSE) (To be completed by everyone)

25. TYPE AND AMOUNT OF CURRENCY/MONETARY INSTRUMENTS		Value in U.S. Dollars	26. IF OTHER THAN U.S. CURRENCY IS INVOLVED, PLEASE COMPLETE BLOCKS A AND B. (SEE SPECIAL INSTRUCTIONS)
Coins	☐ A.	►$	
Currency	☐ B.	►	A. Currency Name yen
Other Negotiable Monetary Financial Instruments Issued in Japanese yen currency	☐ C.	$ Aprox one billion five hundred sixty five million USD value	B. Country
(Add lines A, B and C)	TOTAL AMOUNT	$1,565,000,000.--	Japan

PART IV - GENERAL - TO BE COMPLETED BY ALL TRAVELERS, SHIPPERS AND RECIPIENTS

27. WERE YOU ACTING AS AN AGENT, ATTORNEY OR IN CAPACITY FOR ANYONE IN THIS CURRENCY OR MONETARY INSTRUMENT ACTIVITY? (If "Yes" complete A, B and C)   ☐ Yes   ☐ No

	A. Name	B. Address	C. Business activity occupation or
PERSON IN WHOSE BEHALF YOU ARE ACTING ►	~~COMPLEX INDUSTRIES HOLDINGS, Ltd~~	PO BOX 15580 Newport Beach, Calif. 92659	Research Engineering Financing

Under penalties of perjury, I declare that I have examined this report, and to the best of my knowledge and belief it is true, correct and complete.

28. NAME AND TITLE	29. SIGNATURE	30. DATE
Dr. ~~[redacted]~~	~~[signature]~~	Apr. 27, 89

(Replaces IRS Form 4790 which is obsolete)   Customs Form 4790 (120384)

185

Martin Olson

186

Customs Use Only		DEPARTMENT OF THE TREASURY UNITED STATES CUSTOMS SERVICE	OMB No. 1515-0079
Control No.		**REPORT OF INTERNATIONAL TRANSPORTATION OF CURRENCY OR MONETARY INSTRUMENTS**	This form is to be filed with the United States Customs Service Privacy Act Notification on reverse

PART I - FOR INDIVIDUAL DEPARTING FROM OR ENTERING THE UNITED STATES

1. NAME(Last or family, first and middle)	2. IDENTIFYING NO. (See instructions)	3. DATE OF BIRTH (Mo.Day.Yr.)
███████████		02	05	28

4. PERMANENT ADDRESS IN UNITED STATES OR ABROAD	5. OF WHAT COUNTRY ARE YOU A CITIZEN/SUBJECT?
P.O. Box 15580 Newport Beach, California 92658	USA

6. ADDRESS WHILE IN THE UNITED STATES	7. PASSPORT NO. & COUNTRY
same as above	(USA)

8. U.S. VISA DATE	9. PLACE UNITED STATES VISA WAS ISSUED	10. IMMIGRATION ALIEN NO. (If any)

11. CURRENCY OR MONETARY INSTRUMENT WAS: (Complete 11A or 11B)

	A. EXPORTED		B. IMPORTED	
Departed From: (City in U.S.)	Arrived At: (Foreign City/Country)	From: (Foreign City/Country) Tokyo, Japan	At: (City in U.S.) Los Angeles, Ca	

PART II - FOR PERSON SHIPPING MAILING OR RECEIVING CURRENCY OR MONETARY INSTRUMENTS

12. NAME (Last or family, first and middle)	13. IDENTIFYING NO. (See Instructions) I.D. ██████████	14. DATE OF BIRTH (Mo.Da.Yr.)
███████████████████		

15. PERMANENT ADDRESS IN UNITED STATES OR ABROAD	16. OF WHAT COUNTRY ARE YOU A CITIZEN/SUBJECT?
725 Market Street Wilmington, Delaware	

17. ADDRESS WHILE IN THE UNITED STATES	18. PASSPORT NO. & COUNTRY
P.O. Box 15580 Newport Beach, California 92659	

19. U.S. VISA DATE	20. PLACE UNITED STATES VISA WAS ISSUED	21. IMMIGRATION ALIEN NO. (If any)

22. CURRENCY OR MONETARY INSTRUMENTS DATE SHIPPED	23. CURRENCY OR MONETARY INSTRUMENTS	NAME AND ADDRESS	24. IF THE CURRENCY OR MONETARY INSTRUMENT WAS MAILED, SHIPPED, OR TRANSPORTED COMPLETE BLOCKS A AND B.
Apr. ,09	☐ Shipped To	Complex Industries Holdings Ltd see (15) (17) above JAPANESE POLITICAL TURMOIL REQUIRES DELAY IN PROCESSING (see attach report nbr. 890427)	A. Method of Shipment (Auto, U.S. Mail, Public Carrier, etc.) Courier of ████████████
DATE RECEIVED Apr.29,89	☒ Received From		B. Name of Transporter/Carrier (1) above on Japan Air #62

PART III - CURRENCY AND MONETARY INSTRUMENT INFORMATION (SEE INSTRUCTIONS ON REVERSE) (To be completed by everyone

25. TYPE AND AMOUNT OF CURRENCY/MONETARY INSTRUMENTS		Value in U.S. Dollars	26. IF OTHER THAN U.S. CURRENCY IS INVOLVED, PLEASE COMPLETE BLOCKS A AND B. (SEE SPECIAL INSTRUCTION)
Coins	☐ A. ►$		A. Currency Name yen
Currency	☐ B. ►		
Other Securities & Financial Instruments Issued in Japanese yen currency	☐ C. ►	Aprox five billion USD value	B. Country Japan
(Add lines A, B and C)	TOTAL AMOUNT ►$ 5,000,000,000.--		

PART IV - GENERAL - TO BE COMPLETED BY ALL TRAVELERS, SHIPPERS AND RECIPIENTS

27. WERE YOU ACTING AS AN AGENT, ATTORNEY OR IN CAPACITY FOR ANYONE IN THIS CURRENCY OR MONETARY INSTRUMENT ACTIVITY? (If "Yes" complete A, B and C)	☐ Yes ☐ No		
PERSON IN WHOSE BEHALF YOU ARE ACTING ►	A. Name ████████████	B. Address PO BOX 15580 Newport Beach, Calif. 92659	C. Business activity occupation Research Engineering Financing

Under penalties of perjury, I declare that I have examined this report, and to the best of my knowledge and belief it is true, correct and complete.

28. NAME AND TITLE	29. SIGNATURE	30. DATE
Dr. ███████████	████	Apr. 27, 89

(Replaces IRS Form 4790 which is obsolete)   Customs Form 4790 (12038

Martin Olson

Informing the Japanese Minister of Finance
of the Validity of the MacArthur Fund Japanese Notes

On November 29, 1990 the following letter was sent by the chairman and the Trust to the Minister of Finance (MOF) in Japan outlining the objective of the Trust, the historical background of the Yen Securities and the benefit of Japan and United States of America. General Evaluation.

(November 29, 1990)

Subject:

Yen Securities (hereinafter "Financial Instruments"), dismissed as counterfeit by Deputy Director at Ministry of Finance, Japan, at Government Debt Division, finance Bureau (hereinafter "MOF").

* * * * *

Gentlemen:

Khrushchev delivered the model of Sputnik to the table of President Kennedy at the time, when U.S. had no satellite yet. Until that time and after for nearly one quarter of century the USA taxpayers spent trillion and trillion dollars among others also for the defense of Japan.

188

As interesting historical contradiction is – due to prohibition after the lost World War II. Japan was not allowed to build up military establishment, instead Japan has built up until today, tremendous great industrial and financial worldwide extended admirable power.

However, Japanese nowadays traveling to USA and realize that in USA the common worker has much more comfortable homes, circumstances, than the Japanese at home, regardless from their great international financial power.

Japan, today is a very much contradictory miracle. In one hand she is global power, in other hand most part of the country looks like as an underdeveloped area.

This fact creates a nucleus for social political explosions, what LDP (Liberal Democratic Party) cannot sustain, unless will be eliminated above unbalance.

* * * * *

What to do anything all of this time with the above "subject?" Itself the referred financial instruments were in hands of very amateurish people, whose skill and political education did not reach the level for deeper understanding, that talking about international politics and can be triggered international repercussions, if the referred financial instruments will be used improperly and unprofessionally.

What is the interest of Japan and what is the involvement of USA, regarding these financial instruments? This funny question has very deep historical root. Practical point of view MOF can declare privately that the financial instruments are counterfeit and nave have been issued. However, the present, legitimate holder of the CD's, the Trust do not need to prove that the CD's are genuine. MOF (Minister of Finance) must furnish the prove that the CD's are counterfeit.

The people of MOF are servants of the government and they following the received instructions. However they well understand, that this instruments are in amateurish hands lethal economic and political weapon against Japan. This is why they are stating that there are counterfeit.

Upon unilateral declaration and threat by one or more of the offices of MOF the brokers, middle man, naïve business people in once abandoning further "try," however continuously arriving newcomers, repeating the same.

So during the past several years has been proliferated the actions world-wide to "make big monies" on the financial instruments by this amateurs, all of them on some way approached the same place of MOF. Of course, cannot be blamed the officers of MOF for their "Declarations."

The turning point occurred concerning this above outlined trend, when have been accumulated this instruments in the safe of, in Europe based, very sophisticated, we can say, Trust, under management of the writer of this memo.

It is highly probably, that at top level no one has the complete and accurate detailed information, what is the program of the Trust and what would be the final outcome, if the trust would chose the co-called European Alternative Program (EAP).

I believe, however, that in Japan at top level are inaccurate notions about the organization, headed by the doctor. Must be emphasized, that the Trust made all necessary legal research concerning the history of the referred financial instruments, which going back to the end of the World War II to the period of MacArthur, who worked out the Japanese constitution together with late Emperor Hirohito.

The so-called "Secret funds" which served as financial source for the buildup of the democratic Japan has been turned over to Japanese hands later on by former President Nixon in conjunction wit the Peace Treaty.

It is not the subject of the Trust actions to evaluate whether or not the actions by President Nixon can be legally supported, even in retrospect, or it was some kind of different qualifiable political maneuver.

Our function is, due to the fact that for some, by not us selected reason, we have the destiny to resolve this historical puzzle and place in the books of the history, revising certain already written chapters.

Our motives only in very minor degree driven by desire for money. Of course, we are working, as Capitalistic system used to be for very modest fee.

The Chief motive is to fulfill our historical mission, to manage under tight control the distorted, potentially explosive system and the financial instruments and their economic values deliver back to the place where originally belong.

The existence of the Communist system, in essence, the USSR as Super Power, was the only threat for the Trust to loosing the control about EAP one year ago. It was in that time greater risk, that the financial instruments will be taken over by hostile forces.

Today, above danger does not exist any more.

Under the "New World Order" did remain only one superpower, which is today already historical fact and no one argue any more about this sentence.

The unprecedented UNO actions, among the today expected resolution is the prove, that only USA is in the position to manage the balance on the entire world, for the benefit and security of all nations. This request the highest level of responsible decisions, actions and leadership.

The US Government and the Legislative Body (Congress) working together so closely, which never happened during the past few decades in the US history.

All of this what to do anything with the subject financial instruments?

With patience, it can be understood.

* * * * *

The Trust has completed documentation, based on legal research, made by widely known international exports – concerning the origin of the referred financial instruments. By historical (not yet legal terms) can be furnished unrejectable prove, that the financial instruments represent a long range investment of the US taxpayers, done by historical channels and during a historical period.

The issue is not whether or not the financial instruments are counterfeit (there are genuine), the issue is: What would be the effect to the international political scene, if all questions and answers, relating with M-Funds would go to the international political arena?

The recruit scandal is the prove, that identical origin of financial instruments in amateurish hands how dangerous can be. The Trust will not trigger "recruit scandal" or similar phenomena. The Trust has the function under the laws in and outside of USA to provide facilities and accommodation to resolve this problem definitely.

We have no intention to do favor for the Japanese government, we are not threatening anybody. We are acting responsible and for the interest of USA, consequently for the interest of Japan, too.

We do not have any authorization from the US government. We do not need any authorization from any one.

We are protected under the Constitution of the USA and all of our actions has been and will be executed under the Laws and Regulations.

This is why we do not need to hide anything.

* * * * *

In order to present convincing evidence for top level people in Japan, they must be approached by intellectual methods furnishing the proof that our proposal is genuine and workable, and can be kept under restricted control without any wide and malicious publicity, avoiding all unexperienced and some time unscrupulous brokers.

I outline below in very short terms the so called European Alternative Program in order to convince the proper high, that the already structured "Ready to Proceed" mechanism, which can be in very much details presented by my representative bank officer, is the best solution.

* * * * *

In contrast of, by representative represented mechanics, does exist an alternative program, European Alternative Program (EAC) which is undesirable, however, also workable and has been entirely prepared to proceed in case, may be, the first alternative for some illogical reason will not be accept. It is know, that in Haag exist the International Court, which has no real jurisdiction about any country. The effect of any decision of theirs is rather political declaration, that real verdict, and then cannot be enforced.

However, the international publicity, relating with public hearings, perhaps much more powerful tool in this case, than can be thought.

It is so, that even if some of the representatives of the Japanese Government would be requested to appear before the court as witness, they not necessarily would appear in Haag.

However, the trust has the legal power, based on documentation, that the US Government will consider to send its witness to the International court.

Of course, knowing this factor, the same claim, to be presented at the Haag Court simultaneously will be filed also in Japan at the proper court, requesting the Japanese Government the verification of the genuineness of the financial instruments.

Therefore in Haag, before the International Court will be publicized the same documents, like in Japan at the Japanese Court. This can be achieved very easy, since the constitution in Japan has been drafted based on the US Constitution. The experts who already reviewed the case have not seen any problems about the parallel and simultaneous court procedure in Haag and Tokyo, consequently also in Washington.

It is great deal of naivete to believe that Japan Government is in the position under above mentioned conditions refuse to delegate the witness at Tokyo Court.

It we assume, that some extreme Japanese Group, terrorist, etc., want to kill all persons who managing and assisting this process from side of the Trust, they will not reach the desired result. Cannot be silenced any more the efficiently of the actions anymore, because any, above referred hostile act immediately will trigger the release in different countries already existing complete documentation which will trigger the EAP automatically.

If we assume, that the Doctor will be assassinated, perhaps would be a nice funeral, however, would not change anything regarding the end effect of EAP.

EAP will start with full publicity and the extract of the files will appear in all major capitals in the first page at the most known daily news papers. The EAP would trigger, first of all in Japan the greatest internal political repercussion. Two years ago, before Gorbachev gained his full power, would have been to risky to trigger the EAP, because perhaps Japan would have fallen into the interest sphere of Stalinist type of USSR by help of far leftist communist powers in and outside of Japan.

(Talking about nearly 600 billion dollars value of issued and genuine, existing, controlled instruments, which in essence belong – legally can be proven only by the Trust – to the American taxpayers.)

EAP of course would have very much support from both of the two parties in USA. The Trust relating fees also will be justified and no one will object them.

Our strength is our rationality and objectivity.

If the financial instruments will be confirmed openly as genuine (based on the EAO) would mean, that the trade surplus of Japan would disappear from one hour to the other one. The exponentially. The American industry, business community would applaud to the Trust and only the Japanese population will suffer.

SILENT DEVELOPMENT PROGRAM
SDP

Introduction;

A private Switzerland Trust, which is over 200 years old, is located in Zurich and Lugano and managed by three Trustees of which Dr. Sandor Mihaly is the senior trustee-managing director. The Trusts main function is managing funds consisting of G7 currency and securities and precious metals. Dr. Mihaly is an Scientist, Patent Attorney, Pathologist and Electronic Engineer who has made a decision many years ago to utilize the Trust funds for Medical-Agricultural Research by a complex-detailed planned use of the assets with safety. This detailed plan took over 15 years to digest, refine, educate and staff before starting. Such as the Mustard Seed that is planted, cultivated and is now ready to be in blossom and visible to the need to know. Following is an explanation of our mission.

Mission;

Our mission is to invest Trust assets into worthy large projects globally, with guarantees satisfactory to the Trust, build the project, start the project in an operating condition and turn the completed project over to the proper, agreed upon authorities. The interest and fees earned by the Trust, from each project, will be utilized by the Medical-Agro Research projects. Hospitals and clinics associated with World Health Organization WHO and Food and Agriculture

Organization FAO. Incorporated with the Medical-Agro Research will be an Data Center for the collection of medical-agro information with WHO & FAO that will be made available to all scientists, universities and medical doctors.

Medical-Agriculture

The Medical & Agriculture Research to be known as the DR. MIHALY INSTITUTE of BIO-MEDICINE (DMI) and will consist of a 200 bed acute care licensed built hospital in Palm Beach County, FL. A 100 acre exiting hotel in Lugano, Switzerland that will be converted into an research clinic, a clinic for vaccine testing trails and research in Palm Beach County, FL, an biological-agriculture research facility in Granada and an research office in Wallingford, England. In the future their will be facilities for research in China, India, Indonesia, Philippines and South Africa. All the facilities will be associated with WHO of Geneva, Switzerland and FAO of Milan, Italy.

DMI will have an central computer system that will collect all data globally from every country associated with WHO & FAO, disseminate the data so that scientists, universities, doctors can access for their particular subject as well as, in the future, allow doctors to access the data bank with a patient's symptoms and obtain the best treatment that has been collected globally in the medical treatment field.

The primary subject of the DMI will be in the Gastroenterology field as this is the main starting source of diseases,

YOU ARE WHAT YOU EAT, and Agricultute as it is the energy required by the body and also the source of either a healthy or diseased body.

In the future there will be an Electronic University operating through its central data bank connecting to the various research centers to hold seminars, lectures and courses to the enrolled students for their continuing education as well as advanced studies. With the use of the central data computer center and its connection to major universities, the students will have direct access by video/voice to the activities at the universities and DMI.

This overview of the Medical-Agriculture Research and DMI is only to outline in general terms the broad activity of DMI.

Projects

The financing, construction and project in operating condition is the main source of continuing income to the DMI programs. The financing of selected projects is by the use of trust assets through a complex system associated with central banks and major banks backed by government guarantees approved by the trust. The projects would be such as: nuclear-co-generation plants of 1350 MW or larger, hydroelectric, petroleum and petro-chemical, high speed rail, housing, mining, manufacturing, hospitals and clinics, utilities and et. Most of the projects will be for governments directed agencies with the balance of hospitals, clinics, food processing to be retained by the various entities of the trust. We have studied most of the above projects above in detail and are now ready to implement their start up expeditiously. The engineering will be done by international firms such as Kilborn Engineering and construction will be done by trust entities subcontracting the work. The projects will be in Asian countries, Africa, Mid-East and Eastern Europe with the equipment purchased from Europe, USA, and Japan to start. Enclosed is a chart showing the projects interconnections and the method of the trust to complete the projects known as the Silent Development Program due to the Trust assets and no public involvement in its funding.

Telecommunications

The vital nerve center of the entire program is Telecommunications that will have several activities such as:

1. DMI associated with WHO/FAO
2. Private Banking
3. Trading-currencies, securities
4. Confidential data-shipping, contracts, government documents, insurance, trust assets.
5. Security-travel
6. Projects data
7. Personal data

All the above require confidentiality to insure, as much as possible, the safety of the information. The Trust will lease a transponder and if necessary, in the future, a satellite from Orion Atlantic for global coverage.

Computer-data bank

The brain of the program is the computer. It is estimated that the program will require an estimated 5000 PCs in all 160 plus member countries of WHO/FAO as well as for trust entity offices and project offices. A study was made on the data, past and present on texts, periodicals, reports on medical-agricultural subjects that will be required to be entered into the memory bank of the entire texts or pages. It is estimated that the first 10 years yearly average would be approximately 3,500 million pages with an yearly average after ten years would be approximately 3,000 million pages or an accumulated 10 years of 28,000 million pages and growing. Since today's super computers can perform up to 60 billion calculations per second and scientists now anticipate Petaflops computering a level of performance 10,000 times greater than the fastest of today's machines to solve calculations. This speed will be needed when the program is in full operation and access by the medical field.

Banking

The Trust has formed its own private banking entity known as Euroinvest International Bank & Trust (EUBT) based and chartered in Switzerland. The primary function of EUBT is to manage trade currencies-notes-bonds, trade petroleum-petrochemical contracts, underwrite bonds and manage the assets such as AU/PT as an private bank not handling asnu outside accounts. It is the function of EUBT to have accounts with Central Banks and large commercial banks and brokerage houses. EUBT to open offices in London and Berlin. In the future an office in Singapore. The assets of EUBT to start will be 300 million USD as paid in capital with assets consisting of G7 notes and AU stored in Asia. EUBT solicitor in Zurich will provide evidence-information to our solicitor in London, Linklaters & Paines as required by UK law to proceed with the proper application to the Bank of England. Due to security and confidentiality, the details of EUBT assets will only be given, as required by law, to the proper officials in the Central Banks and proper government agencies. EUBT to have offices in London, Lugano and Berlin and in the future Singapore. Management of EUBT will be from Lugano with its primary office in London. In summary, EUBT is an private bank, managing its own assets, to fund projects of the Trust and to manage the funds for DMI.

14 May, 1994

PROJECTS

ASIA

We have completed detail studies on high tech industrial projects such as the following.

1. Electrical Power Plants

    Co-Generation & Nuclear with transmission & supply facilities.

2. Petroleum Plants

    Crude (Atmospheric & Vacuum)

    Oil refining.   LPGs & Petrochemical feed stock & Synthetic fuels.

3. Petrochemical Plants

    Olefin & Armatics, Styrene, Polystyrene resins, PVC & Polyethylene, Synthetic rubber,

    Methyl tectiary butyl ether (MTBE), Polymes, Solvent Resins, Coatings etc.

4. Aluminum Plants

    Bauxite processing/refining, Alumina sutraction & smelting by the "Bayer Process".

Aluminum ingot for fabrication, feedstock for alloys and compounds.

5. Mining & Metallurgical Industry
    Coal/Precious metal processing plants
    Cyanidation, CIL, CIP process, Ore processing plants

6. Pharmaceutical Manufacturing Plants.
    Generic Y& Patented product manufacturing.

The following projects that are not of high tech nature except for the process machinery equipment required for modern high speed production.

1. Agricultural Products.
    A. Production/processing of Agro products
        (Tomato, legumes, vegetables, fruits etc)
    B. Industrial Crops
        (Cotton, rubber, abaca, corn, soya beans, root crops etc)
    C. Livestock & Poultry
        Beef cattle, hogs, dairy and poultry
        (Meat, eggs, ducks, other poultry species)
    D. Planting material
        Production of breeders & genetic materials

E. Sugar

Sugarcane farms, milling, refining.

2. Fishery & Aquaculture

Purse seining in International waters

Aquaculture – grow-out farm operation, sea-farming, hatchery & nursery.

3. Agriculture/Marine input & service

Slaughter houses & packing plants

Feeds for agriculture

Fertilizers

Veterinary vaccines, Microbial pesticides

Pest & diseases control services

Irrigation & related facilities

Warehouses and post harvest facilities

Fish ports, storage and processing facilities

4. Food, Beverage Plants

Meat processing & canning

Freeze Dry processing, packaging

Fish processing, packaging

Vegetable oil/meal

Corn starch & sweeteners

Confectionery & wrapping systems

Tomato products

Fructose for soaps & sauces

Fine chemicals from food by products

Food chemicals/preservatives

Smack foods

Beverage brewing. Distilling and soft drink manufacturing.

5. Metal Engineering Products

   A. Metal buildings with metal/insulated panels that can withstand 200 mile/hour winds

   (US code) for all proposed plants utilizing modular design for cost efficiency.

   B. Motor vehicle and truck assembly plants

   C. Motor vehicle parts & components manufacturing industry utilizing computerized auto part design.

   D. Ship building, ship repair.

   Ship building facility including manufacturing fishing fleet for more than 100 G.T. vessels.

   E. Aircraft manufacturing & repair

6. Housing, towns and cities.

   Study completed including design and use of material.

7. Textile & textile products

   Chemical fibers and filament yarns.

   Polyester, rayon, nylon, silk, textile dyeing and finishing, cotton products.

8. Research & Development

   Research laboratories/facilities for product development.

9. Public Utilities.

   A. Potable water processing plants for inhabitants, food processing plants, pharmaceutical, textile etc.

   B. Sewage processing plants

   C. Transportation

      Buses, High speed rail, Freight rail system

   D. Inter Island shipping lines

   E. Public telecommunications services

   F. Technology parks, Industrial estates

   G. Port infrastructure, piers, wharves, quays, storage, etc.

   H. Airports – runways, terminals, hangers, electronics, etc.

   I. Hospital – Clinic

   J. Roads – Highways

All the above (not high tech) are needed projects for Asia and are all inter-related and the first priority projects would be:

1. Start of design/build of electrical power
2. Agriculture development
3. Metal building manufacturing facilities
4. Housing
5. All other projects to follow

Because of Asia's great need for all the projects, and whereas EUBT has completed a great deal of research into high tech projects including housing and freeze dry systems, we can speed up the project engineering on many fronts/projects immediately after the government provides all details/sites and size of each project.

EPILOGUE

The constructor of this "Evaluation" is a man with minimal life requirements, his destiny to build up in field of medicine an entire new system to prepare the medical science for the new challenges in the next century for the benefit of our children, for the benefit of other peoples children and for the benefit of the whole human race, regardless from race, color or belonging.

Really do hope that my representative will have the chance to present the concrete program at top level without delay.

The above letter was sent to MOF Japan and as of that date, November 29, 1990, all work has been on hold due to the serious problems of the recession in Japan. The basic problem is the excesses that have occurred in U.S.A. The last twenty odd years and the cleansing of the criminal elements in Japan. This will probably take the balance of the 1990's to be completed.

Since the November 29, 1990 letter which was sent to MOF, Japan, a few more Yen Securities keep popping up by people who think that they can use these instruments as collateral or attempt to cash them in.

One such case came up in Tampa, Florida, in 1992 where people attempted to use these instruments at a well known brokerage house as collateral. These people were picked up by the authorities for attempting to use foreign securities illegally. The U.S. Attorney, with the Secret Service requested the assistance of the chairman on what course they should take as he is the expert. They were told that any attempt to go to Japan would be foolish and would result in nothing as Japan would not disclose any information on the notes. In fact they would be politely handled and the end result is wasted time and could be a stab in the back. Later the U.S. Government formally requested from Japan a representative to testify at a trial in Tampa as to the authenticity of the Securities. Japan refused the U.S. request. U.S. is no man's land. The only action that U.S. can take is find someone that can testify on the notes. There is one person, in hiding and any attempt to bring him out would result in his death before he can be delivered to testify. Again, Japan's ability "way of strategy."

The U.S. Federal counterfeit charges are dismissed without explanation in Tampa, Florida (Tampa Tribune, December 7, 1995).

20 May,1994

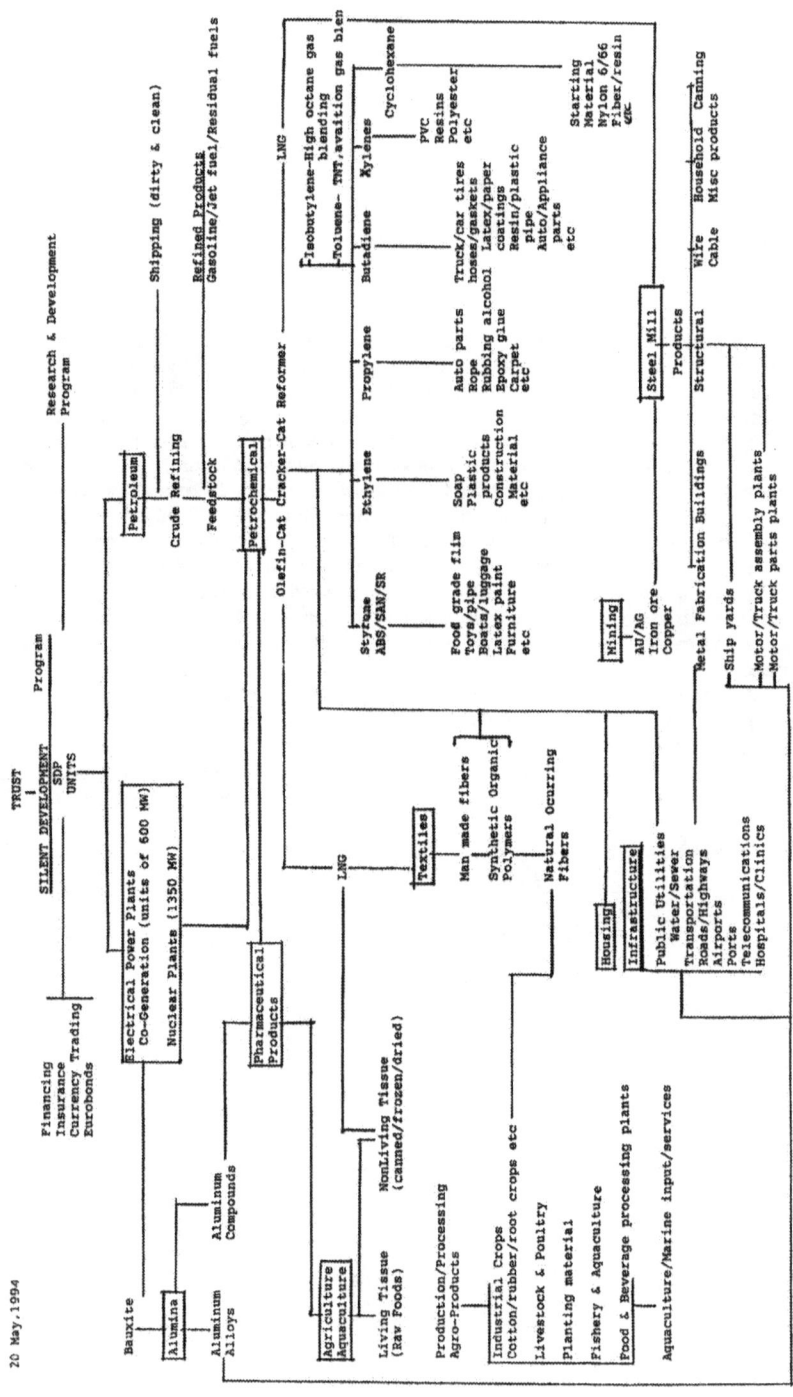

10-09-2001

Dear Martin:

    1.-Thank you for your great fax. Our country now under changes. The people until these time worried only about the money, except the religious good people, like you are. Reckless people under claims of the freedom, have burned the American Flag, to which during the history of the country many blood attached by heros, who fought for our country, like doing today.

    2.- The enclosed map shows where the University will be built. The owner of the property, one on my German Friend will be here on Thursday, adjusting the price of the property, after concluded legal job I will go to Switzerland to let transfer the funds. Overseas is allocated 1.2 billion Europe Dollar Trust monies, for the whole project, from which 70 million for the property has been cleared through the Fed system and the funds are in NY in offshore book entry. Due to the attack in New York, has been introduced worldwide very restricted procedure, whereas every major transaction over about 100K dollars must be processed from the point of origin of fund,(in our case in Switzerland) being in the bank where the person controls the funds by his/her signature, like me. This is logical system, because if I would be terrorist, never would appear in the Bank.

    3.- For the construction of University Complex the former officer of Catalfuno, Mike Taylor got the Director function at Anderson Constructions Company, and he will be responsible the for the construction.

    4.- If you mind, since we will have enough funds for housing, you and (Iris) may ponder to come down to Florida. Her background also may be very useful for some medical activities.

WARM REGARDS, DR.

BIBLIOGRAPHICAL
CREDITS

1.   **Alice in Wonderland**. Carroll, Lewis. 1946.
      Grosset & Dunlap. New York

2.   **Design for Power**. Schuman, Frederick L. and
      Brodsky, George D. 1941.
      Alfred A. Knopf, Inc. New York

3.   **The History of the Decline and Fall of the Roman Empire**.
      (Volume 4) Gibbon, Edward. 1986.
      The Folio Society. London

4.   **MacArthur's War**. Weintraub, Stanley. 2000.
      Simon & Schuster. New York

5.   **World on Fire**. Chua, Amy. 2003.
      Doubleday. New York

6.   **Iron Shoes.** Olson, Martin. 2002.
      1st Books Library. Bloomington, Indiana

ABOUT THE AUTHOR...

Martin Olson was born in New Haven, Connecticut in 1926. He attended public school and later Williston Academy in East Hampton, Massachusetts before enrolling at Yale University. He started his career as a tracer and draftsman, and following an internal drive to build, design and plan developments, became a contractor. He later moved to a position as property manager and consultant for Sears, Roebuck and Company in charge of all development operations on the Eastern Seaboard. Finally, he became a consultant and coordinator to a variety of groups in the United States as well as in the United Nations, and ended up as an assistant to the Chairman of a Swiss Trust.

Martin Olson now lives in Augusta, Maine with his wife, Iris, doing sculptures, wood and granite carvings and sketches. He says, "This is the happiest time of my life. *Iron Shoes* (a reflection on the theme of his first non-fiction book) carried me over the rugged roads to retirement and a chance to share what I have learned in my life with those who must carry on in a world gone mad."

www.ingramcontent.com/pod-product-compliance
Lightning Source LLC
Chambersburg PA
CBHW030310290526
45785CB00001B/294